Congratulations on your retirement, Mike!!

TO A Special SOMEONE

Thinking of You

Have A Nice Day!

floets in W.I.

Kristen Westlake

Curious What's Just Around The Corner?

Here's a brief preview of what you'll find in the pages ahead. This book celebrates the best of Wisconsin...its incredible scenery...and its friendly people.

"IS THERE *any state* prettier than Wisconsin?"

The pictures in this book make a solid contention that Wisconsin is simply the most beautiful state in the nation. For those of us who live here, that case is already closed.

Need photo evidence? You'll find 148 pages of it here. From the comfort of your favorite chair, you can take a tour from the Mississippi River on the west to Lake Michigan on the east...and from Beloit at the bottom to Bayfield at the top.

You'll experience our beautiful seasons...from the promise of spring...the warmth of summer...the color of fall... to the purity of winter. These scenes, shot by some of Wisconsin's best profes-

sional photographers, are so vivid you'll think you're *there*.

We'll take you along backroads you'd likely never see on your own...past pretty farms that exude pride...alongside hidden ponds and quiet bays...and autumn maple trees that take your breath away.

This Isn't Just a "Picture Book". It's far from that. On this "trip" across the state, we'll introduce you to some of Badgerland's nicest people.

You'll read a host of *real stories from real people.* Interesting, upbeat, positive people with something to say and something worth learning.

This book is not so much about a state as it is about the people who live here. Pretty as it is, the very best parts of

Wisconsin reside in the minds and hearts of its residents.

In the pages that follow, you'll read the fascinating stories about their varied interests. Most of it is in their own words, as though they were sitting with you, sharing coffee and a warm conversation.

Much of what you'll see here are selected features and photos from the first 2 years of *Our Wisconsin* magazine. But there's also lots of new items, too.

We pored over *hundreds* of photos and articles to choose only the *best* for this book. It's our hope and hunch that now and then you'll pause and say, "Ah, Wisconsin, we love ya!"

With that, turn the pages and enjoy... *Our Wisconsin.*

Our Wisconsin

Its Beauty...Its Bounty...Its People

There's a Lot of Great Reading Ahead...

Plus These Features...

Our Wisconsin

Its Beauty...Its Bounty...Its People

Editor Roy Reiman
Art Director Sue Myers
Our Wisconsin **Editor** Mike Beno
Copy Editor Kristine Krueger

International Standard Book Number: 978-0-692-29943-2
All Rights Reserved. Published by *Our Wisconsin*,
5602 Broad St., Greendale WI 53129

For additional copies of this book, write to the address above, or call
414/423-3085. Or order online at *ShopOurWisconsin.com*.
Price per book: $18.98 plus $4.98 shipping and handling.
(Shipping is a *flat rate* no matter how many copies you order.)

Pssst! Something's Hidden in This Book!

SUBSCRIBERS to *Our Wisconsin* magazine know we like to add a little fun to each issue by hiding something within the pages, then award prizes to the finders. (It's too involved to explain here; ask a subscriber if you aren't one already.)

So, we decided to add that same intrigue to this book. *Somewhere* in these pages we've hidden a tiny "W". It looks like the sample shown at right. **W** That's not it...the one we hid is much smaller! If you find it, send a postcard or note naming the page where you spotted that W to: *Our Wisconsin*, 5602 Broad St., Greendale WI 53129. Deadline: March 31, 2015.

If you've identified the correct page, we'll then put your entry along with others into our cracker barrel for the prize drawing. Only one entry per person.

What's the Prize? The winner will receive a "Taste of Wisconsin", plus free Culver's for an entire year!

The "Taste" is a *$100 Gift Basket* piled high with sausage, Wisconsin cheddar, Sprecher root beers, dipping mustard and pretzels, fine candies, gourmet nuts, cookies, fudge and more.

And again, the winner receives *free custard from Culver's for a full year*.

If this search sounds like fun and the prize appetizing, look even closer as you study the photos and features in this issue, then enter this tasty contest.

And if you'd enjoy this kind of search regularly in *Our Wisconsin* magazine, see subscription details on page 5. We'd love to visit you every other month through our colorful pages!

"YOU HEAR THAT? That's what this doe likely says every fall as carloads of camera buffs head toward Hayward and other points north when Wisconsin's colorful and peaceful Northwoods beckons. (Ken Dequaine photo)

SNEAK PREVIEW. Tranquil scene at right is just the beginning of the pretty autumn photo tour you're about to enjoy. It shows the Black River burbling through Pattison State Park near Superior. (Terry Donnelly photo)

Have You *Really* Seen Wisconsin?

Have you seen Wisconsin's autumn
With the trees so brightly dressed,
When wild geese go winging southward
And the robins leave their nest?

If you haven't seen Wisconsin
In the autumn of the year,
Then you can never really know
Just why we like it here.

Have you seen Wisconsin's winter
When the snowdrifts pile high,
Where the greens of pines and spruces
Silhouette against the sky?

If you haven't seen Wisconsin
In the winter of the year,
Then you can never really know
Just why we like it here.

Have you seen Wisconsin's summer
Deep in clover and wild rose,
Heat haze dancing on the meadows
Where the cattle lie and doze?

If you haven't seen Wisconsin
In the summer of the year,
Then you can never really know
Just why we like it here.

Have you seen Wisconsin's springtime,
Smelled new lilacs in the rain,
When the fertile land is stirring
And the fields are lush with grain?

If you haven't seen Wisconsin
In the springtime of the year,
Then you can never really know
Just why we like it here.

If you haven't seen Wisconsin—
Summer, winter, spring or fall,
Then you may have been existing
But you haven't lived at all.
—*By Evelyn McLean*

LIKE LOOKING BACK. No TV antennas, no electrical poles, corn shocks in the foreground ...this calm scene captured in the Amish country near Westby offers a glimpse of the past under a breathtaking sky. (Rob Resnick photo)

Wisconsin Autumns Are Awesome!

August through October can take your breath away almost anywhere in Badgerland. The kaleidoscope of colors begins "up north", then trickles down to Janesville.

For so many folks in Wisconsin, fall is the best time of all! Dressed in a rich coat of flaming red, orange and gold, our autumn seasons offer a truly spectacular color show.

The multihued foliage and crispness in the air are early signals that fall is on its way. It's not only the sights but the sounds, such as the crunching leaves below the feet of the postman at right going about his job in the town of Waupun.

These scenes kick off the first of this book's seasonal photo sections...yes, we couldn't resist beginning with fall. So get set for a delightful tour from the comfort of your favorite chair via professional photos so vivid you'll feel you're there!

You'll be startled by the liftoff of migrating waterfowl...hear laughter of kids at play...see apples and pumpkins ripe for harvest...and note red-bellied woodpeckers tapping their tune.

With every page you turn, you'll find something special to like about our state. So get set for a season-by-season tour that celebrates this lovely place we call...*Our Wisconsin.*

John Ford

Mike Roemer

TOUCHDOWN! Isabel Kellner, age 9, celebrates a score during a flag football game in Green Bay. Isabel plays for the Holy Family Comets.

TAKING WING. Wisconsin is a primary breeding state for blue-winged teal, which nest in grasslands. They are early to migrate south in fall, compared to some other duck species.

WALKING HIS ROUTE in Waupun is this friendly neighborhood letter carrier. Photographer Zane Williams, who shot this image, says it reminds him of the simple scenes he used to enjoy in *LIFE* magazine years ago.

Zane Williams

Len Harris

A GOLDEN STROLL is enjoyed by Barb Harris, who walks along a country road near Bell Center—an unincorporated village south of Gays Mills in Crawford County.

Ken Dequaine

Terry Donnelly

RIPE AUTUMN APPLES look like shiny ruby ornaments in this orchard near Galesville in Trempealeau County. There is an abundance of orchards in this west-central region of Wisconsin...many stretch along State Highways 35 and 54.

RED-BELLIED WOODPECKER, photographed near Waupaca, stands out from the maple leaves, but where's the red belly that gives the bird its name? A pink hue on the lower abdomen is seen during spring breeding season. These birds are common in Wisconsin and winter here; any migrations are short in distance.

Ken Dequaine

Jack Roper

CRIMSON CRANBERRIES float in the flood that was put onto their beds at this farm in Wisconsin Rapids, which is home to some of the largest cranberry marshes in the country. Short, teasing bursts of frost before harvest help give cranberries deeper color. But growers vigilantly use sprinklers to guard against an early hard freeze that could wipe out an entire crop. Wisconsin is the top state for cranberry production.

TURKEY SHOOT? Only with a camera! Photographer Jack Roper encountered these birds as they crossed a road in Oconto County. Wild turkeys hatch in Wisconsin in May or June, and juveniles remain with the hen into fall. Growth of juveniles ends by winter.

TOUGH TO TOP is the view on the next page, where Holy Hill is dressed for autumn. This shrine to St. Mary is one of the state's most famous landmarks. Its location on a high kame is one of the tallest points in southeastern Wisconsin. (Jeffrey Phelps photo)

Allen Blake Sheldon

Linda Freshwaters Arndt

THE FALL COLORS come from more than leaves in the village of Pepin. Car clubs annually take autumn rides in their vintage vehicles up State Highway 35, the Great River Road.

WHERE BAD IS GOOD. This breathtaking overlook of the Bad River (right) is seen at Copper Falls State Park located near Mellen. This popular park welcomes visitors all year-round.

AUTUMN IN SPRING? Spring Green, that is! In this Sauk County village, you will find pumpkins by the wagonload at Peck's Farm Market. Thanksgiving and Halloween are near!

Mike Crowley; next page: Clint Farlinger

A CHEEKY CRITTER is the least chipmunk, common in far northern Wisconsin. Its larger cousin, the eastern chipmunk, is abundant statewide. With bulging cheeks, this chipmunk will probably transport the food to its burrow.

Wisconsin TRIVIA

Things You May Not Know About Our State

Did you know the exact center of Wisconsin is 9 miles southeast of Marshfield?

Here's a trove of trivia to sprinkle into your conversations that your friends might find interesting.

YES, the geographic center of Wisconsin is pinpointed at latitude 44°26.0'N and longitude 89°45.8'W in Wood County, 9 miles southeast of the town of Marshfield. As a result, Marshfield is known as "Hub City".

THE SUN rises and sets 22 minutes earlier each day in Sturgeon Bay, the east edge of the state, than in Prescott, 310 miles away at the west edge.

THERE ARE badgers in the state, but not enough to be considered pests. Wisconsin earned its "Badger State" nickname not because of an abundance of badgers, but rather because early settlers who worked in the numerous lead mines either lived in mine shafts or dug their homes out of the sides of hills...as furry badgers do.

A REAL BADGER is difficult, if not impossible, to dislodge from its den. Their tunnels can go down more than 12 feet and be over 50 feet long. They've even been known to tunnel through asphalt!

RIVER RUNS THROUGH IT. Wisconsin is named after its longest river. Wisconsin is the English version of *Ouisconsin*, an Indian name for the river that runs 430 miles through the center of the state.

WE'RE BIG. Wisconsin encompasses 65,503 square miles, including more than 15,000 lakes and 33,000 miles of rivers and streams. Wisconsin ranks 23rd in size of the 50 states.

THERE ARE 982,155 acres of water in Wisconsin, which represents 2.6% of the state.

LEGENDARY FALLS. At 165 feet, Big Manitou Falls in Pattison State Park, near Superior, is Wisconsin's highest waterfall and is the fourth largest falls east of the Rockies. Six of the state's 10 largest falls can be fond on the outskirts of Hurley.

BRRR! The lowest temperature in Wisconsin ever recorded was -55°F at Couderay (Sawyer County) in 1996. The highest temperature recorded in Wisconsin was 114°F in Wisconsin Dells on July 13, 1936.

RAINED BIG TIME. The most precipitation in a single day was 11.72 inches at Mellen (Ashland County) in 1946.

LARGEST INLAND LAKE is Lake Winnebago, covering 215 square miles and 131,939 acres. The deepest lake in the state is Green Lake, with a maximum depth of 236 feet.

SUPPER CLUBS began popping up in Wisconsin in the 1930s. Milwaukee native Lawrence Frank is credited with opening the first one (in Beverly Hills, California) in the 1920s.

HIGH THERE. The highest elevation in the state is Timms Hill in Price County. It's 1,951.5 feet high and located about 25 miles west of Tomahawk.

CASHTON is home to Wisconsin's largest Amish community, with about 300 families farming in southern Monroe County. Wisconsin has the fourth largest Amish population in the nation.

THERE ARE 50 state parks in Wisconsin that cover a total of 60,570 acres.

WE'RE NUMBER 1. Well, at least we were —Wisconsin was the first state to number its highways. For what it's worth, Interstate 43 is actually an intrastate, because it does not cross Wisconsin state lines.

THE RINGLING BROS. CIRCUS originated in Baraboo in 1884.

DOOR COUNTY is among the top cherry-producing regions in the U.S., with more than 2,000 acres of cherry orchards.

OLDEST CITY in Wisconsin is Green Bay, founded as a trading post in 1634.

THE HONEYBEE is Wisconsin's state insect. It collects pollen from 50 to 100 flowers on an average day, and it takes about 2 million flowers to make 1 pound of honey.

STATE SONG: *On Wisconsin*. State Flower: Wood Violet. State Tree: Sugar Maple. State Bird: Robin. State Animal: Badger. State Wildlife Animal: White-Tailed Deer. State Dog: American Water Spaniel. State Fish: Musky. State Rock: Red Granite. State Motto: Forward. State Dance: Yeah, you betcha—da polka.

WATERTOWN was the location of the country's first kindergarten in 1856. Its first students spoke German.

SAD RECORD. The Great Peshtigo Fire in 1871 has the distinction of causing the most deaths by fire in American history. While more people died in the terrorist attacks of September 11, 2001, technically it was the collapsing buildings rather than the flames that killed most of the victims.

"M'WAUKEE." That's how many Wisconsinites pronounce Milwaukee. And " 'Scansin" for Wisconsin is common, too ...as is "Yah hey" as an affirmation.

THE WORLD'S largest carousel is the one at the House on the Rock in Spring Green.

AL CAPONE liked to fish, and in the 1920s he had a retreat near Hayward. He had a fieldstone lodge built there with 18-inch bulletproof walls.

ARNOLD SCHWARZENEGGER earned a degree in business administration from the University of Wisconsin-Superior in 1979. He became a seven-time Mr. Olympia winner in addition to an actor and governor of California.

IN APRIL 1973, the Brewers season opener was delayed 4 days after a 13-inch snowstorm blanketed Milwaukee.

BLUE AND GOLD PACKERS? Yes, the colors of the Green Bay Packers were originally blue and gold. The green uniforms were issued in 1950, and the green and gold tradition began.

CHEESY EXPLANATION. Wisconsinites are known as "Cheeseheads". The nickname surfaced in 1985, when the Chicago Bears won their first and only Super Bowl, and their fans attempted to ridicule their northern neighbors. With the Packers' record and dominance over the Bears since then, most residents now wear the Cheesehead proudly. Go, Packers!

Jess Burg

What We Love About Wisconsin

When we began planning this book, we asked Our Wisconsin readers to share what they loved most about our state. Here's a sample of a boatload of responses.

"TO ME, Wisconsin is among the breathtaking areas of God's creation. Its rolling hills, farm fields, lakes, streams and rivers all offer moments of relaxation and nostalgia. Wisconsin is a life-affirming experience!" —*Claire Engelbart, Milwaukee*

"HERE'S what Wisconsin means to me: **W**hen **I**n **S**cenic **C**ountry **O**bserve **N**ightskies **S**unsets **I**rresistible **N**ature." —*Cathy Wheeler, Glenwood City*

"MY HUSBAND and I feel extremely fortunate to have been born and raised in the Upper Midwest. But when we were able to retire in Algoma, just a half block from Lake Michigan, we felt we'd won the lottery!" —*Rhonna Hemm, Algoma*

"FOR ME, you aren't really in Wisconsin until you go 'up north'. You have to get beyond Wausau to fully understand and appreciate why the Indians so loved this state.

"The streams, the small lakes abundant with fish, the hills, the woodlands, the pines—just the scent of those pines is so appealing, they should make a cologne from it! I love all of Wisconsin...but I love it even more up north."

—*George Westly, Burlington*

"WHAT is Wisconsin? It's beer, cheese, the Packers, up north, Friday night fish fries, Harley-Davidson, wildflowers in summer, snowdrifts in winter, and proud people who care." —*Linda Schumacher, Edgerton*

"I LOVE that Wisconsin is 'home' for me, and I revel in the memories: Summer weeks at a cottage on a lake up north...visits to Wisconsin Dells...riding the Hiawatha train to Wausau with my mother...delivering newspapers in the snow at Christmastime...helping bale hay and harvest potatoes on my in-laws' farm in Marathon County...watching our kids chase chickens there...learning to polka...seeing grandchildren experience the beauty of the Kettle Moraine. For me, memories are made of this." —*Vern Borth, Wisconsin Rapids*

"WISCONSIN gives me the 'blues and the B's'. Blue streams, bluebirds, blueberries, blue skies and blue jeans. Big red barns, bass, bears, boats, birds and bats, Bucks and Brewers, and, of course, brandy and beer." —*Linda Reed, Burlington*

"WE'RE SO GLAD to be back. We lived in Texas for 18 years and finally moved back 'home'. We love the four seasons and knowing when they arrive.

"I love getting up in the morning and hearing birds singing and seeing deer in our backyard. We also have a couple of bears that like to make an annual appearance.

"Above all, we're glad to be back where the air is clean and healthy to breathe."

—*Hazel Petersen, Black River Falls*

"I ENJOY the wonderment of Wisconsin that I experience right in my own backyard: watching 'Henrietta', the wild turkey, appear several times daily with her 10 kids...hummingbird moths that miraculously appear in July while the phlox is in its glory...Mr. Cardinal, who speaks to me from a shrub branch a mere 3 feet away... and the feisty squirrels who know my visit to the feeder means a new food supply.

"It's obvious many pairs of eyes are watching me each day. All of these thrills are evident in our wonderful Wisconsin." —*Mae Salow, Waukesha*

September Is Simply Spectacular!

As proof, many who now reside in other states drive or even fly "back home" in late September. The seasonal show is just too good to miss.

By September, summer has ripened into the first stages of the rich golden autumn days that follow. This dramatic change in the seasons is one of the best things about living in Wisconsin.

Soon, locals begin checking fall color reports to see where the hues are at their peak, then pile the kids in the car for a drive in the country.

We all love the color, of course...the brilliant yellow aspens, the blazing red maples and golden tamarack spires against a deep-blue sky.

But we love the aromas of September as well. We pick up whiffs of freshly made sauerkraut, tart apple cider and a just-baked pumpkin pie.

Then there's the sound of delighted neighborhood kids playing in the leaves, and the yells of adults when the Packers score!

For the sights, sounds and scents, it's when everyone here wants to be outdoors. Yes, September in Wisconsin is simply spectacular!

Clint Farlinger

Bob Firth

COLORFUL AND TIDY FARMSTEAD is located near Maiden Rock, a historic railroad and river settlement on Lake Pepin in Pierce County.

PINING FOR A HIKE? You'll come across an easy and relaxing one in this red pine plantation along the Scuppernong Trail. It can be found near Eagle, in the Southern Unit of the Kettle Moraine State Forest.

CACTUS BLUFF (right), at Ferry Bluff State Natural Area in Sauk County, affords a fantastic view of the Wisconsin River. (Tom Algire/Larry Ulrich Photo)

Denver Bryan

BEST BIRD-HUNTING BUDDIES. Andy Cook of Sister Bay and his yellow Labrador retriever, Pip, take a well-earned break during their grouse hunt. You'll often find the pair roaming the woods near their hunting camp at Armstrong Creek, in Forest County.

John Ford

WIDE WINGSPAN of 6 to 7 feet carries sandhill cranes to and through Wisconsin. In fall, migrating cranes stage by the thousands in wetlands such as Crex Meadows, White River Marsh, Sandhill State Wildlife Area and Necedah National Wildlife Refuge.

COTTONTAIL RABBITS are common in the south and central parts of the state. They've expanded their range to northern counties, where snowshoe hares traditionally dominate.

John Ford

Mike & Marshia Crowley

ROOM WITH A VIEW. Majestic eagle and young eaglet were photographed in their tree nest on High Lake in Vilas County. Eaglets grow at the rate of 1 pound every 4 to 5 days. By 3 weeks of age, they measure about 1 foot tall, with feet and beaks that are nearly adult size.

STATE ANIMAL. According to the Boone and Crockett Club, Wisconsin's the top state in the U.S. for trophy deer hunting.

istockphoto.com

John Ford

FAMILY FARMS remain common in Wisconsin. There are 12,100 licensed dairy farms in the state, making Wisconsin the leader in cheese production.

23

ROUND BALES of hay can weigh up to 900 pounds. "Views like this are so common in Wisconsin that we drive by without giving them a thought," says Carol Toepke, who shot the idyllic rural scene near New London. "I always like to slow down to appreciate the labor and bounty of Wisconsin's farmers."

GOLDEN GLOW. Called a "wild canary" by some folks, the common goldfinch brightens summers here in Wisconsin. This one was photographed in a garden near Greenwood.

John Ford

Mike Roemer

TAKE A TASTE! Elke Roemer of Green Bay shares an ice-cream cone with her dad, John, outside Dippy's Ice Cream Shop on Founder's Square in Fish Creek, one of The Door's popular destinations.

SERENE SUNSET. Windmill stands near Mineral Point, a Driftless Region town named for the minerals easily accessible near the surface. Cornish immigrants mined here in the 1930s.

Rob Resnick

Jeff Halverson

COMMANDING VIEW. Perched atop a pine tree along the Turtle Flambeau Flowage in Iron County, this majestic bald eagle has a perfect spot to watch the water for its next meal.

Aaron Peterson

GRANDVIEW ORCHARD near Antigo offers 50 varieties of apples, ready picked or pick your own. Orchard tours are conducted and an apple fest happens the first weekend in October. There's cider, honey, jams and Amish goods available. What a spectacular spot for a late summer-early fall excursion!

Carol Toepke

HOOFIN' IT. Pig races are one of the unique events at the Wausau Hot Air Balloon Rally and Glow. Kids of all ages cheer on their favorite porky. Winner gets an oatmeal cookie!

TALL SHIP WINDY, from Chicago, sails through the Sturgeon Bay Ship Canal from Lake Michigan to Green Bay during the Tall Ship Festival in 2013. Windy was one of seven tall ships that raced from Chicago to Green Bay for the event. The Tall Ship Festival will return to Green Bay as its host city next in 2016.

Carol Toepke

Carol Toepke

Kristen Westlake

WING WALKER Teresa Stokes performs in the Gene Soucy Air Show at the EAA AirVenture in Oshkosh. She's a pilot, stuntwoman and a talented artist, who designed the paint scheme on this plane. EAA AirVenture happens each summer.

CROSS-COUNTRY MEET was held in Whitewater, where Kristen Westlake was shooting the action.

GREAT GRAPES. Lautenbach Orchard has produced fruit on 100 acres near Fish Creek since 1955. It's home to a winery, cider mill and farm market. Cherries, apples, raspberries, pears and more are sold there. Wine tours and tastings are offered as well.

Shana Shoblaska

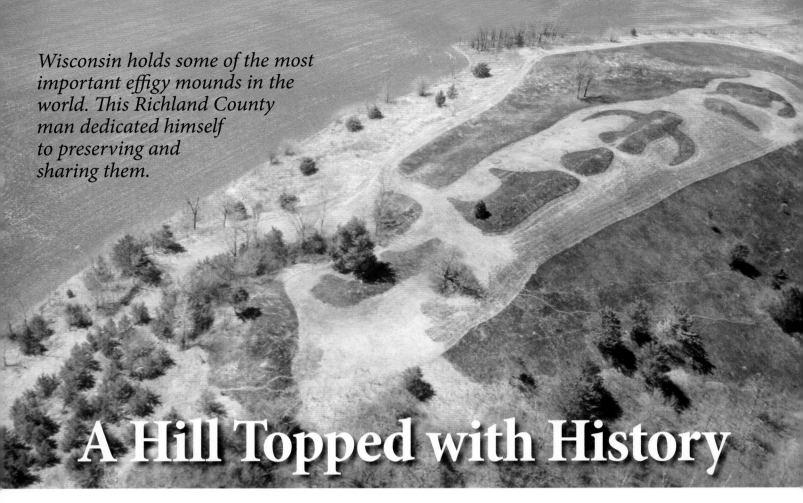

Wisconsin holds some of the most important effigy mounds in the world. This Richland County man dedicated himself to preserving and sharing them.

A Hill Topped with History

By Kevin Schoenebeck, Platteville, Wisconsin

"ISN'T THIS a beautiful view?" Though he's stood here a thousand times before, Frank Shadewald still marveled at this commanding overlook of the Wisconsin River Valley from high atop his windswept hill in Eagle Township, 12 miles south of Richland Center.

Eagle Township

Yes, it is a spectacular sight.

Wooded ridges rise steeply from the valley floor below. Farm fields fit neatly between the ridges like simple square puzzle pieces. Serpentine creek beds and patches of wetlands are scattered amid the fields. Water towers indicate small towns in the distance: Muscoda, Blue River, Avoca and more.

But what's most amazing about your visit to Frank's Hill is not the matchless view. It's right at your feet.

Along the top of this ridge is a series of low earthen berms shaped as animals by Native Americans centuries ago. "It's a remnant of the largest cluster of effigy mounds in the world," says Robert Birmingham, recently retired state archaeologist of the Wisconsin Historical Society.

"Frank's Hill is absolutely unique and important because the effigies here are so well preserved."

Between A.D. 700 and 1100, Native Americans built more effigy mounds in Wisconsin than anywhere else in North America. An estimated 1,300 of these sizable earthworks were sculpted in the shapes of birds, mammals and other figures by different native civilizations across the centuries.

Farming and industry destroyed 80% of the original mounds. Those that remain hold mysteries about the people who made them and why.

According to Birmingham, the effigies were formed as animals that symbolize Native American clans. Birds, bears, bison and serpents are most common.

Images of Their Ancestors

"These are visual images of their religion placed right on the ground," he explains. "They are supernatural animals in the belief systems of native people—literally an image of their ances-

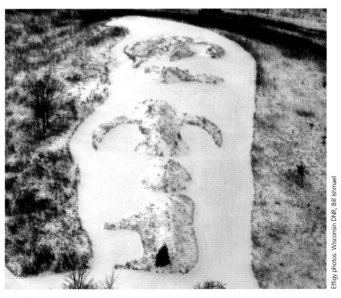

Effigy photos: Wisconsin DNR, Bill Ishmael

A DUSTING OF SNOW makes the effigies stand out in stunning relief. Frank's meticulous mowing and weed burning keep them distinct.

tors. They believe they are directly descended from these animals.

"This is so interesting to me," Frank says, guiding you on a tour of the mounds as his old dog Annie trots happily at his feet. "Here's the plumed serpent," he says, pointing to a berm in the ground. "It's one of the original gods going back to the Mayans."

A few yards away he points out a beaver, bison and coyote, all strung neatly along the spine of this ridge.

One large effigy appears to be a bird, which Native American visitors have told Frank symbolizes the "Corn Woman". Legend credits this god for providing the seed and knowledge for her people to grow crops that sustained them.

As a retired grain farmer, Frank understood something about that. And he felt a strong connection to this land and the people who lived here centuries before.

Educated as an engineer, he embarked on a decades-long career related to rural electrification. Then from 1972 through the early 1990s, Frank grew grain in this rural neighborhood and taught engineering at Fennimore Technical College.

HIGH ON A HILL is Frank Shadewald and sidekick Annie. He fastidiously tended his property to preserve Native American effigies.

His interest in archaeology blossomed as he discovered a series of conical mounds on his farm.

Archaeologists used ground-penetrating radar to confirm 24 graves within those mounds. As the scientists visited, so did Native Americans from many states. The Ho-Chunk wanted to preserve the property, so in 1994, he sold his farm to the tribe.

Frank and his wife continued living at their home adjacent to the farm, but it wasn't long before he jumped back into archaeology as a landowner.

In 1998, a neighbor offered Frank the 120 acres that includes the effigy mounds. His long-suffering wife thought they were done with all that science and the never-ending visitors.

"My wife was always against this stuff," Frank said. "But then when the land came up for sale, she told me to buy it. That just about floored me."

Kept in rough pasture for years, Frank's Hill was overgrown with thick grasses and has little agricultural value. So each spring he burns the hilltop to control weeds. Then he mows meticulously around the mounds, about five times per growing season.

Visitors from Around the Globe

Frank hosted visitors from all over the world at Frank's Hill. He invited groups annually to experience sunrise and sunset on solstices and equinoxes.

"When you stand at the head of the Corn Woman during an equinox, the sun appears to rise directly in line with her," Frank said last year. "It looks as if she's giving birth to the sun. There are creation stories tied to all of this.

"One spring when some Native Americans came to help me burn, I told them, 'Maybe you want to scatter tobacco and ask the Great Spirit to spare us from this fire getting away from us.'

"Their leader said a prayer in his language. When he finished, we turned around and saw three bald eagles, nearly motionless, hovering on a thermal above us. Then they were gone. Our burn went well and we were safe that day."

He Feels a Connection

Calling Annie back to his red pickup, Frank pointed out a secluded spot a few yards away from the effigies. He'd like to clear some more brush, mow a little more and expand it as a quiet area for reflection.

"I want this to be a peaceful spot where people can relax and be near all this creation," he said. And he has some thoughts about planting prairie grasses and wildflowers.

"I've dedicated myself to this," added Frank, as he closes the gate to the parking area and turns the truck for home. "This is sacred ground and I truly believe that."

"This is a wonderful part of North American history right here in our state," archaeologist Birmingham says.

"I admire and respect Frank for working so hard to preserve it and keep the stories alive. Frank Shadewald has been a great friend to Wisconsin history."

HUMBLE HANDMADE SIGN stands near this poor patch of pasture. Today this land is recognized on the National Register of Historic Places.

Editor's Note: Frank Shadewald passed away in 2013, shortly after this article appeared in *Our Wisconsin* magazine. Prior to that, he'd established the nonprofit Three Eagles Foundation, Inc. For information, or to make a charitable contribution, call 608/739-3079.

window on
WISCONSIN
Favorite photos shared by readers.

Stadium Seating?
Hunter Lake in Sawyer County is a long way from Lambeau Field or Camp Randall. But Mike Phelps of Rockford, Illinois captured this campsite scene there, as set up by some real sports fans.

Dave's Falls...in Fall
"A beautiful place to visit during autumn is Dave's Falls Park in Marinette County," reports Teri Standiford of Porterfield.

View's Fair in Eau Claire
Nancy Coddington of Eau Claire snapped this autumn photo of the Eau Claire River from a vantage point downtown.

Smirking Chipmunk

"We sat for over 10 hours taking photos of chipmunks and birds one day and found this delightful one in the mix," says Shell Foeckler of Superior. "This chippy seemed to be smiling and has become popular in our family."

Now That's Saying Something

"Shiloh, who lives in Manawa, seems to enjoy showing off for the camera," writes Danae Bauer from Scandinavia, in Waupaca County.

Tranquil Scene

Catherine Erickson captured the view of fields and hills (below) near her home in Prairie Farm. With a population of 473, the village is situated near the Hay River in Barron County.

Mom's Li'l Pumpkin

"On a beautiful fall day, my husband, Shawn, and I decided to take 3-month-old Porter to his first pumpkin patch," says Cindy McDonough of Howard. "Porter was patient for the 'photo shoot'."

Shots to Share? If you have a photo that captures the beauty of Wisconsin or the fun in living here, send it to: *Our Wisconsin,* 399 S. Hwy. 51, Manitowish Waters WI 54545. Or e-mail to: *editors@OurWisconsinMag.com* and put "Window on Wisconsin" in the subject line.

AUTUMN ON FIRE. Glowing larches ring this tiny unnamed lake in Vilas County, where photographer Mike Crowley loves to fish in fall...as much for the color show as for the potential of a good catch.

A Blond and Her Boat?
This Guide's No Joke

*Move over, guys, this petite angler has hauled in hundreds of muskies—
and rowed hundreds of miles to do it.*

By Patricia Strutz
Eagle River, Wisconsin

WHEN I WAS just 6 months old, my parents took my sister, brother and me camping "up north" in the Nicolet National Forest. Each summer after that, we visited Lac Vieux Desert and Seven Mile Lake.

It was on these waters that I learned to swim, water-ski and fish. Who'd have guessed that years later I'd guide folks to their first big musky right here?

My husband, Jim, and I, both from the Appleton area, moved to Eagle River and I caught the fever...*musky fever.*

"Musky fishing" conjures images of big, burly men hurling oversize plugs for endless hours as they hunt an elusive sport fish. I hurl those same lures, only I'm a 5-foot-3 woman. Funny thing is, the muskies don't care. They'll equally bite— or not bite—my lures.

Donned Captain's Hat

Encouraged by some male guides, I decided to don a captain's hat and establish my own guide service called "A Blond and Her Boat". (Yes, I've heard all the blond jokes.)

The first year, 100% of my clientele were men. That was fine—I'm the proverbial tomboy who can hang with the guys. But it did start me on a mission: to get more women involved in fishing.

Today well over half my clients are female. Through the years, I've met some amazing father-daughter duos, husbands and wives, sisters and girlfriends. Several single mothers have even asked me to teach them to drive a boat so they can

FIRST MUSKY. Client Lisa hoists the biggest fish she ever caught. At right is Patricia, whose mission is to introduce many more women to fishing.

take their children fishing. I truly believe the future of the sport depends on getting more women involved. If mom wants to fish, then so will the kids.

I'm pleased to say I've seen the tides turn. When I used to drive up to the boat landing, I was an oddity. The guys just gawked and snickered. Now they don't bat an eye.

My favorite method to catch muskies is called "row trolling". It's using manpower to drag lures or live bait enticingly behind a rowboat.

This is an old-school style of fishing, but it's effective. Back before high-powered boats with trolling motors, all Northwoods fishing guides used this tactic.

Casting Needn't Be Costly

I've taught many men and women how to "work the oars". This is another of those *the-fish-don't-care* scenarios. The muskies don't care if you're in an old rowboat or an expensive powerboat. They can't tell a Cadillac from a Smart car.

And I've learned this: Row trolling appeals to fishermen and women who prefer

peace and quiet. Rowing a boat around a beautiful lake is rewarding in itself.

Add in the chance to catch the king of freshwater fish, and it just doesn't get any better! (Motor trolling, by the way, is illegal in northern Wisconsin.) Rowing is environmentally friendly. And rowboats can access many more small lakes where fish haven't seen much pressure.

You don't have to be a power lifter to row troll—I'm 100 pounds soaking wet. It's just not as hard as it looks—the boat is designed to do most of the work. I've caught hundreds of muskies row trolling.

A Real Fish Story

One of my favorite fishing stories predates my guiding days.

I was launching my old rowboat next to a couple fellas in a beautiful, expensive Ranger. They were eyeballing me and my rig. I could hear the snickers and their learned discourse: "What does this broad think she's doing?"

A short time later, I rowed past them on the lake and my rod bent. *Fish on!*

I hauled in a nice-size musky, snapped a quick photo with my self-timer and then released her to fight another day.

The fellows just stood there with their mouths open—speechless—and fishless.

I'm still grinning.

Northern Wisconsin remains one of the top places to catch "the fish of 10,000 casts". Whether you row troll or cast, whether you're male or female, I urge everybody to wet a line.

Maybe you'll catch the fever, too. At the very least, you'll capture cherished moments and hours of fond memories.

Patricia Strutz can be reached via her Web site, *pstrutz.com.*

Eagle River

CHEESEHEAD Has Aged Well

From a wild idea created on a whim, this cheesy headgear is whey more popular than its originator imagined.

By Roy Reiman

HEAD CHEESE MAKER. Ralph Bruno's golden idea went to his head, then to millions of others'. Now he has two new items for the other end—soft cushions called "Sit Mitt" and the "End Zone" (see below).

THIS GOLDEN WEDGE has started numerous conversations between complete strangers. Whether at a football game in Florida or a tailgate in Toronto, "You're from Wisconsin, huh?" is the opening line when someone's "Game on" togs are topped off with a Cheesehead.

This slice of Wisconsin has been spotted—and worn—by Badgerland fans in about every corner of the world. It's displayed in the Smithsonian Institution...has been seen on a shelf in a *Cheers* episode...saved a life in a plane crash...and reached its pinnacle when a hiker carried one along when he climbed Mt. Everest.

Nothing could have been further from Ralph Bruno's mind when he was reupholstering his mother's couch back in 1987. If you haven't heard the story, here's a cut of this hat's history:

Ralph's always been great at fixing things and was doing his mom a favor before heading to a Brewers game with a few of his fun-loving buddies. As he pulled part of the gold foam cushion from the innards of the couch, an idea suddenly struck him.

He'd heard of Wisconsinites being referred to, somewhat disparagingly, by our neighbors to the south as "cheeseheads". So, what if he cut a wedge of this stuff and popped it on his head? That should get a reaction from his friends!

"I cut the foam into a triangular shape, then used a wood burner to poke some holes in it," Ralph recalls. "Mom wasn't too happy because her kitchen started smelling like burned plastic."

Parking Lot Embarrassment

With a bit more shaping to make an opening at the bottom for his head, Ralph popped it on and hurried to County Stadium. "Honestly, it took a little guts to get from the car to my seat, because people were pointing and laughing at me," he says.

"And when my friends saw it, they kept blinking in disbelief.

They didn't even want to sit by me! But all through the game, people kept asking me where I'd bought it.

"'Bought it?' I thought. '*Bought* it?' By the end of the ninth inning, I was convinced it had potential."

A business was born that day.

It took Ralph 2 weeks to get the first one ready for sale. As demand grew—and grew—he improved the product and the process and made more. Eventually, he opened a plant in St. Francis called Foamation, where today he and his crew keep cranking out all sorts of cheesy creations.

Ralph doesn't want to put a number on how many Cheeseheads have been sold...nor did he mention if he ever finished his mother's couch. But sales are likely well over a million, since they're sold by mail, phone, online and in gift shops far beyond Wisconsin.

Most Badgerland fans love them. But there are some who wince at this wedge, feeling it projects a hickish image. Love it or loathe it, the Cheesehead has become a slice of Wisconsin history.

Cheese, It's a Lifesaver!

Frank Emmert Jr. of Superior gives this hokey headgear credit for saving his life. In 1995, as a passenger in a light plane, he realized he was about to crash and grabbed something soft to protect himself. "It saved my face and my arms...and likely my life," he says.

Today the Cheesehead has aged well and continues to be Foamation's top seller. But the firm also turns out a host of related products such as coasters, car dice, drink holders, footballs, earrings, ties and more. There are even earplugs about the size of a golf ball...for horses.

Ralph and his creative staff have come up with a couple items that could match the Cheesehead in potential: They've launched a seat cushion in the shape of a baseball glove called a "Sit Mitt", and another in the shape of an overinflated football called the "End Zone". (See the cushy samples at left.)

The latter two items, which can be produced in the color of any team, may have them sitting on another success story...which means they'll have the market covered top to bottom.

Let's All Let Out a Big 'Aah' for October!

It's okay, too, to say "aah" when scanning the photos on the pages ahead.

Wisconsinites get in a bit of a hurry in October. It's understandable ...there's just so much to see and do before we all ease into November's nip and its pull-up-the-cover nights.

The color of the Northwoods beckons, so October's when carloads of nature buffs begin hurrying to Hayward and beyond. For those south of Wausau who are willing to wait, it won't be long before those blushing orange hues creep down to Tomah, Barneveld and Beloit.

A wordsmith once described autumn as a second spring, when every leaf becomes a flower. That aptly describes October in Wisconsin, with its explosion of color from the River to the Lake.

At this time of year, we watch the forecasts so we can sneak in one more picnic and family barbecue. Yet, we know it's also time to think about getting the boat out of the bay.

But no one's in a bigger hurry than Wisconsin's farmers, who are at it early on frosty mornings harvesting corn, soybeans and a last cutting of hay for cows to munch during the months ahead.

Here and on the pages ahead are images from some of the state's top photographers who love to share their favorite fall views.

Eileen Herrling

POLLY'S PUMPKIN PATCH near Chilton was where this barn cat happened to leap into view. Eileen Herrling took the photo, then picked out a pumpkin to take home and carve.

Christine Schlosser

John Ford

REGAL ROOSTER. Rich autumn sunlight wams this ring-necked pheasant. These birds often emerge from grass and brush to the field edges to take some sun as the weather cools.

MANN, WHAT A VIEW. "This image is of Mann Lake in the Northern Highlands State Forest of Vilas County," writes Dave Miess of Oregon. "It was a beautiful day, and the colors were fantastic." This 253-acre lake has a maximum depth of 18 feet, and visitors can access it through state land and a public boat launch.

AUTUMN STROLL. Page Tierney and Cory Schlosser of Wausau enjoy a walk across the bridge at Fern Island Park in Wausau. The park is known for its many stone bridges and interconnected walking trails. This scenic setting on the Wisconsin River is popular for wedding ceremonies. Together with Oak Island Park, Fern Island represents 27 acres of green space in downtown Wausau.

MAPLE LEAVES sprinkle color across the fender of a 1934 Plymouth. The car has 50,000 miles on it and still runs. It's owned by Richard Loeb of Sullivan and has been in the family since 1965. Richard works as a blacksmith at Old World Wisconsin in Eagle.

FOREST FLOOR FLASH. "I was hiking on a beautiful autumn afternoon near Rustic Road 60 in Vilas County when I spotted these brightly colored mushrooms," says Nick Bristol of Lone Rock.

Jack Roper

Nick Bristol

RUN TO DAYLIGHT. A Winneconne player runs for yardage against Omro in The China Bull Game. This high school rivalry dates to 1948. The schools play for a traveling trophy called The China Bull.

Jim Koepnick

Eileen Herrling

Shirley Bradley

GREAT DAY FOR A RIDE! Eileen Herrling of Appleton was photographing fall color off Highway 17 in northern Wisconsin when she spotted this curve. "I had to stop for a photo here and was glad this biker came into view."

FLOATING PEACEFULLY. A yellow maple leaf adds color to the blue surface of Roberts Lake near Crandon. "When conditions are right, I like to sit on the dock and try to capture the fall leaves as they drift by," says Rob Resnick of Oshkosh. "When the leaves drop, they float upon what appears to be a liquid sky."

Rob Resnick

KIDS AND CRUNCHY LEAVES...a great mix. "Our grandkids were having fun raking leaves and jumping into the piles," says Shirley Bradley of Denmark. We think this says "autumn in Wisconsin".

INVITING AVENUE... for an autumn stroll on a sunny day along Lake Superior, enjoying the season's best colors on Manypenny Avenue in Bayfield. (Bob Firth photo)

AT HOME IN DE PERE. It was clearly cold near the Fox River on the day of this photo, but Kurt, Ellen and Jane Lyon felt the warmth of home.

Home's Where The Heart Is

There's truth in that old saying, as this wayfaring Wisconsinite came to learn.

By Kurt Lyon, De Pere, Wisconsin

De Pere

IN 1990, my wife, Jane, and I moved to Wisconsin with our 9-month-old daughter, Ellen. On the day we arrived in De Pere, the first question from the neighbors was, "Are you Packers fans?"

No, we weren't. We were native Iowans. And we'd lived in four Midwestern states before moving here.

But it didn't take long to become Packers fans. And we also became fans of Wisconsin—and living here taught this native son of Iowa an unexpected lesson.

Jane and I were born in central Iowa, and I grew up on a dairy farm near Toledo. Established in 1927, the farm was worked by my father and his brother...with 22 kids between them. All of us worked there.

I earned a degree in dairy science at Iowa State. Jane and I met there, married, then headed off to work—in South Dakota, Missouri, Ohio and finally Denmark, Wisconsin, where I took a job at Land O'Lakes Dairy Co-op.

Jane enjoyed her work as administrator and religious education coordinator at Resurrection Catholic Parish. Daughter Ellen thrived at school in De Pere, the only home she knew. In 2007, Ellen graduated from De Pere High School and headed to UW-La Crosse. Jane and I loved our home, but did we really need three bedrooms? Our jobs, friends and church were here, but our extended family wasn't.

I'd always thought that someday I'd "go back home" to Iowa. Back to family and the farm, where I'd work again with my brothers and cousins.

In 2010, my father-in-law became ill, so Jane and I made many trips back to Iowa to see him in his last weeks. Sixteen

---

> *"I've never figured out why Wisconsin has more bratwursts than Iowa..."*

---

hours of round-trip driving gave me time to think about the meanings of home.

Iowa's corn and bean crops were beautiful that fall, and the small towns glowed of good economic times. Perhaps I was hearing the call to go home.

Just 6 months later, my mother died suddenly, so back to Iowa we went. Neighbors helped our family celebrate her life with the comfort and welcome only a hometown can provide. Iowans' friendliness and helpfulness were in full bloom. Again, I felt the call to return home.

It Was Decision Time

So we made the big decision. I took a job in northwest Iowa while Jane would remain behind to oversee our home sale.

I rented a house in Iowa and started a new job. It was going as well as a new one can, but every couple weeks I'd get a call from friends at the old office. Just checking in, they'd say. And they wanted to know where something was, and...oh, by the way...we haven't filled your position yet.

Months went by with no offers on the house. Jane continued at the job she loved for 17 years. In Iowa, I kept getting those calls from the old office. I had to admit, Iowa didn't feel the same anymore. At least not the way I saw it in my memory.

I was hearing the call to go home, but that call was coming from Wisconsin. It was then I realized "home" was where I'd been for the last 22 years. So I went home for good.

Having lived in both states, I can tell you that an Iowa ham sandwich is great, but it's much improved with a slice of Wisconsin cheese. One thing I've never figured out is why Wisconsin has so many more bratwursts than Iowa, which produces more pork. Maybe it's due to the festive atmosphere in Wisconsin.

Both States Have Benefits

As an example, Milwaukee and Des Moines both host great state fairs. But Milwaukee is famous for beer and motorcycles while Des Moines is known for ethanol fuel and life insurance.

People in both states are Midwestern friendly and helpful. In Iowa, when your tractor gets stuck in the mud, neighbors pull you out and expect nothing in return.

In Wisconsin, I've heard, one farmer got his tractor stuck the evening before he had to go out of town. The next day, his neighbors pulled it out but left the exhaust pipe standing alone in the mud hole. The farmer returned home believing his tractor had sunk out of sight!

Wisconsin seems to have that added festiveness I've come to enjoy. So we're here to stay. And if the rumblings of another midlife crisis ever begin, I'll address it the Wisconsin way.

I'll get a Harley.

The Prettiest Farm
in Wisconsin
This Outagamie County property really rocks.

By Tina Gohr, Kewaunee, Wisconsin

CARL AND KAREN Vanden Heuvel never met a rock they didn't like…and according to Karen, that caused her dad to conclude they had rocks in their heads.

You see, Karen's dad, Joe Van Wyk, was the second generation in the family to run this Outagamie County dairy farm in the town of Oneida. When Joe's parents bought the property in the 1890s, it was totally wooded, and that meant clearing.

They grubbed out stumps and hauled countless stones to clear crop fields…and every spring after the frost left the ground, up came a new crop of fieldstones. "I don't know if my grandparents used stoneboats and horses to clear those fields," Karen says, "but they had a lotta kids."

Oneida

Karen picked her share of rocks as a youngster. So did her future husband, Carl; they grew up just a mile apart. Eventually, these Seymour High School sweethearts

PILED HIGH is the limestone "escarpment" where Karen and Carl get a view of their property. Gazebo above, built in 1982, is flanked by bubblegum petunias and marigolds.

A STONE'S THROW from the house is a rock garden, where dwarf conifers are interspersed with petunias, celosia and black-eyed Susans. Fieldstones were formed into a 5-foot-tall pyramid. Tranquil garden path (far right) is mulched with white pine needles.

Photos: Karen Vanden Heuvel

married and took over the Van Wyk farm. With them came some new landscaping ideas.

"Farmers *hate* rocks," Karen explains. "When Dad heard I was hauling rocks *back* to the yard, and asking all the neighbors for their rocks, too, he said, '*Are you crazy?* I spent years getting rid of stones, and now you're hauling them all back?'"

Yup.

The result turned into a stunning garden of plants, trees—and rocks—that would rival a page out of *Better Homes and Gardens*. This farm has been featured on two garden walks and was one of five garden destinations for the Midwest Regional Hosta Society's annual convention in Green Bay in June of 2014.

Meet the Flintstones?

Carl and Karen's "quarry garden" is a 2-1/2-acre hobby that began in 2001. "Growing up, we hung out in nearby quarries," relates Karen. "They were our swimming holes." So the couple decided to go with a quarry theme for their extensive garden.

With help from their sons, Joel and David, they moved and arranged 800 tons of rocks and boulders. These were set in and around a 30- x 15-foot pit dug 4 feet deep by a friend who bartered excavating services for spruce trees.

They relocated the large rocks with a 1929 Manley wrecker boom. The apparatus was originally used to hand-crank cars from ditches. They also used an old inherited tractor.

The process was painfully slow. It took 5 years to build the quarry garden, and the work, of course, is never done. Thankfully, most of the bullwork is complete, and that suits Carl just fine. "We're getting older and those rocks are getting heavier!" he says.

The Vanden Heuvels grow more than 500 varieties of hostas and plant more than

2,000 annuals among the rocks with a spattering of natural and heirloom plants. Neither Carl nor Karen is a Master Gardener, but you wouldn't know it during a tour of their property—both reel off plant names as easily as reciting the alphabet.

Built Their Own Greenhouse

They've saved a quarry-full of money by propagating cuttings and planting from seed in a greenhouse that they built. The couple got out of farming some years ago, and a neighboring farmer now rents their fields. Carl is a metal fabricator and Karen is a housewife…a very busy one. Because they still own the land, they maintain it, and that's nearly an occupation in itself.

"It's amazing how long it takes to tidy up," says Carl. "You start at one end, work your way to the other end, then start all over again," Karen laughs.

Inside the farmhouse, there are colors to rival the gardens, as Carl and Karen have found time for their new hobby: creating stained glass. Their lamps are inspired by Tiffany, and windows are styled by nature.

With such incredible color on this property, it isn't surprising that wedding photographers seek the spot for bridal parties, and garden clubs log it on their lists of sites they'd like to visit.

What's the best part about this unique garden? "Whatever is blooming at the moment," quips Carl. "It changes every day."

The Vanden Heuvels are avid readers of *Our Wisconsin* and welcome visitors to their farm to see the flowers in bloom. They can be reached at 920/228-0072.

THE QUARRY POND is the main feature on the beautifully landscaped property. It's 50 by 75 feet in size and planted with water lilies. Below, Karen visits with her hen-friend Tina at the chicken house.

Pow WOW!

Here's your chance to experience the pageantry of dancers from 28 tribes. It's a spectacle to enjoy.

DANCERS above are in the "Men's Fancy Dance" category. Little one at right is a "Jingle Girls' Dress Dancer".

By Jim Leuenberger, Shawano County Field Editor

THE FIRST WEEKEND in August is a colorful time to visit Menominee County—in some ways even more spectacular than when its hardwood trees turn crimson and brilliant gold in autumn.

That's when the village of Keshena hosts the Menominee Nation's Annual Powwow, which is held at the historic Woodland Bowl.

If you've never attended an Indian powwow before, this is the one you shouldn't miss!

Contestants and spectators travel from across the United States and Canada to be part of the dance and drum competitions held all weekend long. In 2013, 447 dancers representing 28 tribes from 14 states participated, making it one of the largest powwows in the nation.

More than $80,000 in prizes are awarded, with dance competitions held in several age categories: tiny tots (ages 1-5), juniors (ages 6-12), teens (13-17), adults 18-49 and adults over 50.

"Our event is like a homecoming since so many of our members relocated to seek employment years ago," says Joan Delabreau, powwow chairperson.

"Most who left were from 18 to 45 years old. Succeeding generations return on powwow weekend to keep in touch with relatives who remain on the reservation."

Memories are rekindled and new friendships are made amid the live drumming, singing and dancing. The theme for the 48th annual powwow, in 2014, was "Dancing With Our Ancestors".

The "grand entry" is among the most spectacular events you'll ever see, as all of the costumed dancers march and perform simultaneously on their way into the bowl.

In addition to the competition, vendors are on-site selling traditional Native American crafts, beads and powwow fabrics. Plenty of luscious foods are available, including both contemporary fare and a variety of Native foods to try.

Briana Ninham, recording clerk in the Menominee Tribal Chairman's office, says, "The difference between our powwow and most others is that we have the contests incorporated into our event.

"While traditional powwows are mostly intra-tribal events to honor family and communities, ours focuses on bringing everyone together from many tribes. This showcases the different dance styles and drum groups.

"Due to the prize money, we attract the best of the champion dancers and drummer/singers. It makes the Menominee Nation Powwow a spectacle you won't soon forget."

For information, contact Briana Ninham at 715/799-5114, ext. 1267; or visit *www.menominee-nsn.gov.*

Keshena

IT'S A COLORFUL COMPETITION!
The first full weekend in August, hundreds of competitors flock to Keshena from tribes across North America to compete in the dance contests in several categories. Just some are shown here. Boy at top left is part of the Boys' Fancy Dance. At top right, a competitor awaits her turn in the Women's Fancy Shawl Dance. At lower left is a contestant in the Teen Boys' Grass Dance, and at lower right, another in the Women's Fancy Shawl Dance.

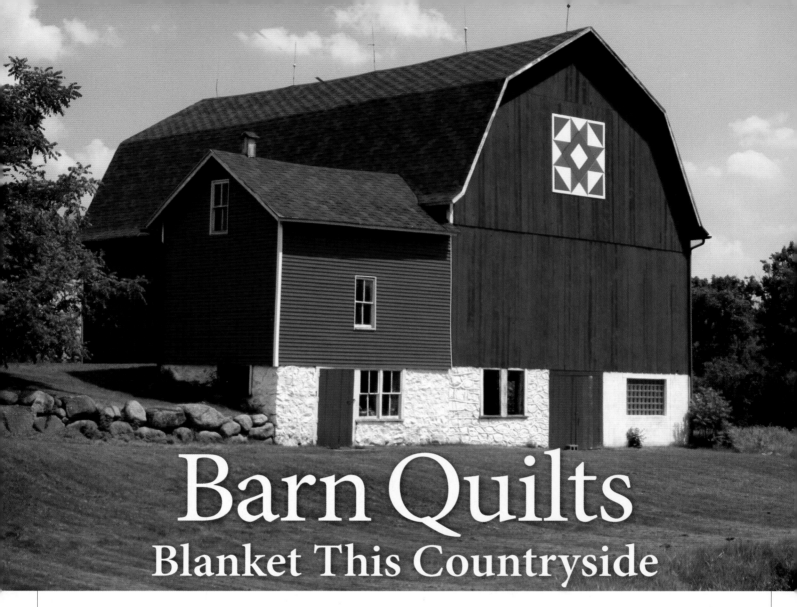

Barn Quilts
Blanket This Countryside

Volunteer project adds beauty and warmth to northeastern-Wisconsin landscape.

By Jim Leuenberger, Shawano County Field Editor

A DRIVE through Shawano County is a lot more colorful than it used to be. That's due to hundreds of brilliant "quilt blocks" displayed on barns throughout the county. If you've recently driven Highway 29 between Wausau and Green Bay, you know what I mean.

I started this "quilted barn" project here after seeing such works proudly displayed in Iowa, Kentucky and other states. The idea is to dress up a barn with a unique piece of artwork, much like a fabric quilt block. The pattern and colors are custom-tailored for each barn owner.

Shawano

Originally I hoped to get 40 to 50 quilted barns. But that goal has been far surpassed—a total of *276* barn quilts are now on display from Wittenberg on the west end of the county to Pulaski on the east.

The project not only encourages preservation of the historic barns in Shawano County, it also gives visitors another reason to come to our area. Many people are now taking a leisurely drive to see these quilts. Here's how the program works: Barn owners can spon-

sor their own quilt, or an individual or business can sponsor one. Either way, the barn owner chooses the pattern and colors.

Many people in the community have pitched in to help. For example, 4-H clubs and other local groups painted about 20 of the quilts. My wife, Irene, and I painted many of them on a volunteer basis to keep costs low. Just $200 covers the materials and costs to display each of these 8-foot-square artworks.

Painted in Basement Studio

The Shawano Country Chamber of Commerce has been kind enough to provide basement space for painting. The program has also had a lot of support from our local newspaper, the *Shawano Leader*, which publishes an article and photo on each quilt. Feedback from the community has been gratifying.

Sharon Hoffman and her husband, Lee, sponsored the county's 17th quilt, which they helped paint and proudly display on their barn in Shawa-

ADDING COLOR to Shawano County is a quilt block called "Card Basket" (top). It's located at the Reeder Farm in Eland. At left is the "Compass Star", which is proudly displayed at the Schneider Farm.

no. "We felt a spark of interest when we first heard about the project," Sharon says. "After seeing a few quilted barns, we knew this was something we'd like to do. It helps preserve our Wisconsin farming heritage and beautifies our byways at the same time."

A Project with Heart

Eldor and Pat Erdmann, also of Shawano, chose to leave their mark on their property with a patchwork heart design.

"We saw this pattern and it made us smile," Pat says. "When we must leave this farm—which we love so much—we'd like to think our hearts will always be here through this beautiful quilt."

The Woven Hearts quilting group of Tigerton has sponsored four quilts to date. "Barn owners who've received these quilts have been so appreciative," says member Audrey Nelson. "It makes us feel good to support such a wonderful project."

Neighbor Peggy Miller adds, "As a quilter, I've always loved the idea that our fabric works bring warmth and comfort to those who receive them. Sponsoring barn quilts is a whole new way to share the beauty of quilts while drawing attention to our county's beautiful barns."

One of the most poignant patterns features the POW/MIA symbol. It's on a barn owned by Vietnam vet Mike Wright, several miles west of Shawano on Highway 29, and was sponsored by local eye doctor Bill Stern. The quilt pattern is called "You Are Not Forgotten".

How many barn quilts will we eventually display? I'm not sure, but Shawano County is 500 square miles in size with literally hundreds of barns, so the sky's the limit. Now that we have accomplished displaying over 275 of them, as far as I know, we have more 8-foot-square barn quilts than any in other county in the United States.

But it isn't my project. It's something our entire area has embraced, from business owners to individuals to the barn owners themselves.

Working together has generated feelings as warm as Grandma's quilt. Come to Shawano County and feel the warmth.

For information on every barn quilt, along with a map showing the exact location of each, go to *shawanocountry.com* and click on the Barn Quilts icon.

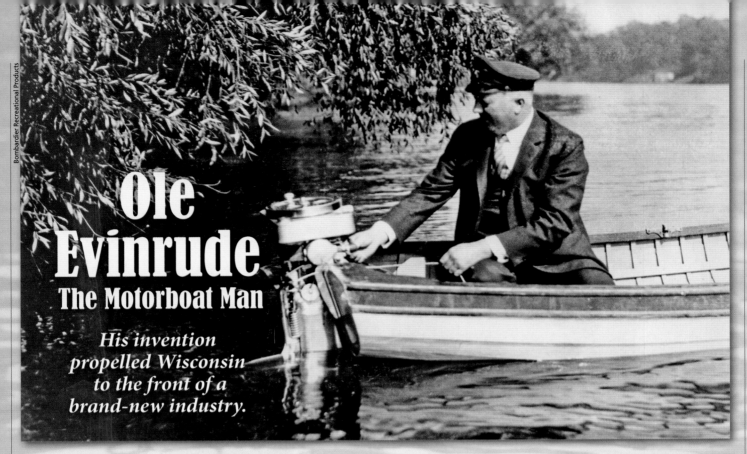

Ole Evinrude
The Motorboat Man

His invention propelled Wisconsin to the front of a brand-new industry.

By Mike Martin, La Crosse, Wisconsin

OLE EVINRUDE'S fascination with boats began at an incredibly young age.

In 1882, when he was only 5, his parents booked passage on an ocean liner from Norway to America. Later, his mother and grandmother recalled that on the trip across the Atlantic, it was nearly impossible to keep Ole out of the ship's engine room.

The family settled in Cambridge, Wisconsin, where Ole's father, Andrew, tried his hand at farming. By age 10, Ole was working on the farm full time and already displayed a knack for fixing equipment.

But boats were Ole's first love. At age 15, he built a sailboat he hoped to sail on nearby Lake Ripley. This project had to be kept secret from his father, because Andrew had lost three uncles to accidents at sea back in Norway and hated boats.

When Andrew discovered Ole's first boat, he tore it apart and burned it in the woodstove. Undeterred, Ole built another —though he hid his second attempt better.

When this 18-foot sailboat was finished, Ole put it in the water. This time his father conceded defeat, telling the boy he had "built a right nice boat". It proved to be a moneymaker, as Ole gave rides to tourists all summer, making as much as $5 a day.

Worked as a Machinist

This money helped pay Ole's rent that fall when he moved to Madison to work in a farm machinery shop. He soon became a crackerjack machinist, hiring out to work at shops in Chicago and Pittsburgh, too.

In 1900—still only 23 years old—Ole moved to Milwaukee to work for the E.P. Allis & Company. Allis made steam-powered machinery, but Ole was more intrigued by the new internal combustion engines.

Between 1900 and 1908, he came up with countless gas engine designs and even

---

"Don't row! Throw the oars away!"

---

built his own automobile—a carriage powered by a smoke-belching engine. He entered a number of partnerships to form a car-making company, but all ultimately failed because the partners did not get along or were poor marketers.

During these years, Ole fell in love with a neighbor girl he'd hired to do bookkeeping. He and Bess Cary were married in November of 1906.

The story goes that earlier that summer, when Ole and Bess were picnicking on Okauchee Lake, Ole rowed across the lake to get Bess an ice-cream cone, but it melted before he made it back.

That disappointment got him thinking about designing a motor to fit on a rowboat. Ole completed his first outboard motor in 1909. He knew he had a winning idea the Sunday afternoon that the motor was demonstrated on Pewaukee Lake. Not only did someone buy it on the spot, but 10 other people ordered one.

The Demand Grew

Bess, who turned out to be an excellent marketer, put ads in the Milwaukee newspapers that read: "Don't row! Throw the oars away!" Sales skyrocketed for Ole's invention. By 1913, his company had 300 employees and was selling nearly 10,000 motors yearly.

In 1914, Ole sold his share of the company for what would be more than $3 million in today's dollars. He got back into the outboard motor business in 1920, when he designed a revolutionary lightweight aluminum motor that was 50 percent more powerful than previous motors.

In 1929, Ole became president of a corporation called OMC (Outboard Motor Company), but when Bess passed away in 1933, he was devastated. He died a year later in Milwaukee at age 57. OMC thrived into the 1980s under the leadership of Ralph Evinrude, Ole and Bess' only son.

OMC was bought out of bankruptcy in 2000 by the Canadian company Bombardier Recreational Products.

Today, all Evinrude motors are built in Sturtevant. The motors' basic design is so good that it's little changed from the first one Ole Evinrude built 105 years ago.

Not bad for a Wisconsin kid who never made it past the third grade.

Cabin Fever

The simple life suits her fine in Manitowish Waters.

N"NOW THAT I live in the Northwoods year-round, I can't believe how much I love fall and winter," says Tara Nolan of Manitowish Waters.

Tara grew up in Marion, Wisconsin, and summer weekends were spent at her grandparents' place on Rest Lake in the Manitowish Chain. "Summer was the only season I knew here, but the serenity in the other seasons was something I never realized…and something I needed."

It took a long time for Tara to value this serene lifestyle, having worked for years on the corporate fast track. Her sales position in finance and marketing demanded nearly all her time.

She had a home in Milwaukee and an apartment in Chicago. She was promoted several times and reached upper management at an early age.

Tara's fast-paced career became so all-consuming that she didn't even recognize it. "The job brought financial success," she says, "but the trade-off was a stressful life.

RELAXED and refreshed is Tara Nolan at her special place in the woods. Tall red pines and maples surround her cozy cabin on the Manitowish Chain of Lakes in Vilas County.

NORTHWOODS DECOR with an Eastern touch reflects Tara's tastes. She grew up vacationing nearby, but her world travels have brought touches of Asia to her home. Modern, efficient kitchen fits her needs. Living room windows from a supper club impart an old-time feel.

Today, I no longer see that as true success." Battling burnout, the young executive took a sabbatical. Little did she know it would change her life.

In 2007, Tara took a year off and traveled the world. She toured South America, Australia, New Zealand and Southeast Asia. Though she hadn't set out to do it, she ended the journey with a month of intensive training in yoga and eventually became certified as an instructor.

Found a Quieter Life

"I'd done a little yoga in Milwaukee, but never understood the spiritual side of it. Most people think it's just an exercise, but it's more. It's a way of life…and when I came home, I wanted a different life."

Tara returned to the family place on Rest Lake and spent a summer instructing yoga classes. "I thought to myself, I'm so happy living here, and I'm so happy doing this, why not do it full time?"

That led Tara to a new career…and the cozy cabin she loves today.

"I wasn't necessarily looking for a log home, but this place seemed so artistic. It felt warm in the way the original owners had incorporated so many different wood grains. When I walked in, I instantly knew it was my dream."

SERENITY AT LAST. One of Tara's first home projects was to add her "yoga deck" out front. Here, this instructor holds classes in a natural setting. The patio makes a fine place for a cool drink on a warm day.

Tara's cabin isn't big, and that suits her. It was built in the mid-1980s by Bob and Joan Poggi, using trees cut from this site.

"I met them after I moved in, and they pointed out the sizable beam in the living room. They'd carried in that huge log together."

A number of vintage treatments were incorporated into the construction, including windows that came from a former resort. As a result, "People always remark that the place looks older than it is," Tara says. "I've kept much of it as it was, but I've done some remodeling to make it my own."

Tara added her "yoga deck" out front, which is just one of the places she holds classes. "The natural setting brings a feeling of deep relaxation and peace," she says. "Deer are walking past us when we're out there."

These days, Tara teaches up to 15 classes per week—at her cabin, at a studio and in homes. "People often gather a group of friends and hire me to provide instruction in their homes," she says. "Many are on the chain, a few are on the islands. I sometimes take a boat to work, and that's awesome!

"Traveling around the world taught me this: Northern Wisconsin is truly one of the most beautiful places to be. Here I've found a sense of peace, joy and fulfillment."

IRON COUNTY CASCADE. Near the town of Gurney, the impressive Lower Potato River Falls is the convergence of three rivers. It can be seen from a county park that's easy to find. (Aaron Jors photo)

Ready?
...Here Comes Winter!

No getting around it—Wisconsinites are a hardy bunch. Many look forward to winter...enjoying the "purity" of snow and finding the cold "invigorating".

When the first flakes begin fluttering, you can almost hear a host of Badgerlanders saying, "Bring it on!" For them, winter is welcome, and the brave love it brisk.

This season's beauty is hard to deny when a crisp, clean blanket of snow adds a sparkle to the landscape, making everything look white and new. As one wag put it, "Even everyone's lawn looks great!"

Little wonder the kids can't wait to get outdoors to build a snowman or snow fort or start a good old-fashioned snowball fight. Adult outdoor lovers look forward to activities such as snowshoeing, cross-country skiing or just a simple hike. A solid surface crunching below your feet allows you to trek most anywhere during wintertime, even on lakes (and there are no mosquitoes!). Then you head indoors for some hot chocolate.

Winter's a nice time of year to simply relax. After the end of an active winter day, there are few things better than sitting near a crackling fire to enjoy a little reading. And you can do that now in the pages here and ahead—welcome to a Wisconsin winter wonderland!

Mike Crowley

'SNO JOKE, he loves the Pack! "I'm always thinking about the Packers," admits Mike Crowley of Boulder Junction. That's why he and his wife, Marshia, decided to build this spirited snowman.

CHRISTMAS ON THE MARCH. The Green Bay Southwest High School Marching Band performs in the annual holiday parade in downtown Green Bay. Nine marching bands, over 20 decorated floats and giant balloons are commonly part of this parade. The 2014 event was the 30th annual.

Mike Roemer

Carol Toepke

SEE YOU IN SPRING. Photographer Carol Toepke says this birdhouse in Fremont gave her a cozy feeling despite an icy day. It awaits the return of the songbirds, just 4 months away!

A VIEW WEST from the Lake Superior ice caves (at right), captured on Mawikwe Bay near the town of Cornucopia. (Jeff Richter photo)

Bickwinkel/Alamy

BARN IN BRILLIANCE. The warm rays of an afternoon sun make this sturdy dairy barn stand out against the snowy landscape near Sturgeon Bay.

Mike Roemer

YOUTHFUL COMPETITORS are among the 9,000 skiers who participate in the American Birkebeiner, the largest cross-country ski race in North America. The marathon is from Cable to Hayward, but there are shorter races, too. The "Birkie" is held each February. For info, check *birkie.com*.

COLD DUCK. Ducks do head south for the winter, but mallards will remain in relatively large concentrations across southern Wisconsin. This hardy breed can withstand all the cold that a Wisconsin winter can dish out, as long they have open water available to them. (Brian Wolf photo)

John Ford

Clint Farlinger

WINTER WAXWING. A handsome bird, the cedar waxwing is migratory. Some flocks remain all winter, especially around Milwaukee and Madison.

FIT FOR A KING. A warming fire and hot drink await a contestant at this checkerboard on a lazy winter afternoon.

CALM AFTER THE STORM. A winter storm had just rolled through near Oshkosh when Rob Resnick caught this beautiful scene on the following pages, silhouetting a sturdy tree and farm against the setting sun, topped with puffy clouds.

MARATHON FOR MUSHERS. The Apostle Islands Sled Dog Race, held annually north of Bayfield, hosts competition in four divisions. Longest is the 8-dog 80-mile race, covered in 2 days. Amenities include bonfires, concessions and spectator warming tents. Check *bayfield.org.* (Joann Will photo)

John Ford

DINING, NOT DORMANT. Raccoons do not hibernate, but go into winter dormancy. They interrupt it to seek food as temperatures near 32 degrees.

Aaronpeterson.net/Alamy

SUPERIOR EXTERIOR. A family explores the outside of the colorful ice cave formation on Mawiwke Bay, seen on page 57.

PIKE THROUGH THE ICE. These "hard-water fishermen" have successfully located the hot spot to catch a few northern pike on this frozen lake.

SMILE FOR THE CAMERA? No problem here, as Autumn Peissig holds little Bridget Cloud while coasting downhill near Colby.

AN EARLY TASTE OF SPRING. You know winter's losing its grip when spring crocuses start pushing through snow. Crocuses are part of the iris family.

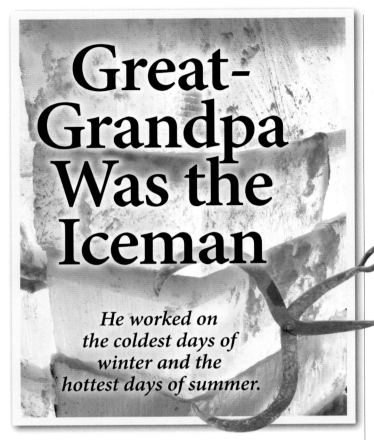

Great-Grandpa Was the Iceman

He worked on the coldest days of winter and the hottest days of summer.

By Juli Relford, Cumberland, Wisconsin

BEFORE the days of refrigeration, everybody used an icebox to keep their food fresh. That meant ice was needed in homes from spring through fall.

Wisconsin's clear and abundant lakes were the perfect source for this ice, which was cut, packed in sawdust and stored in sheds, where it kept right through summer.

The winter ice harvest was an important enterprise during the early 1900s, a cold, tough job tackled by the hardiest of men. In Cumberland, Wisconsin, the local iceman was Tom Alfonse—my great-grandfather. (That's Tom in the photo below right.)

Tom bought his ice business in 1917 from George Miller, who'd started it in 1903. It was located on Beaver Dam Lake, a winding body of water that nearly surrounds town, which we call "the island city".

January through mid-February was the best time to harvest ice, when it thickened from 18 to 24 inches. Temperatures of minus 30 were common then. Sharp tools, strong horses and an experienced crew were needed to bring in the ice.

Scraped Off the Snow

Grandpa Alfonse started the job by clearing some snow off the lake near his home. With a horse-drawn scraper, he'd clear a patch 120 by 200 feet—more total area than a football field. After repeated scrapings, he had a patch of clean blue ice.

He then etched a large checkerboard pattern onto that ice using a horse-drawn plow. The plow had seven teeth spaced 24 inches apart.

To make the checkerboard, the plow was pulled down the length of the ice patch, then across its width. The plow was drawn over these rows six or seven times, until the grooves were 7 inches deep. This could take up to 5 days.

Then the sawing started.

A corner cake was hand-sawn on two sides, then chiseled out. Each cake in that row was chiseled and lifted out. When a row of cakes was removed, the men could break off the entire next row.

Individual cakes measured 24 by 24 inches and weighed 150 to 200 pounds. With pike poles, they were floated to a wooden chute that extended from a flatbed sleigh.

Heavy tongs gripped the cakes, which were pulled up the chute and onto the sleigh by a horse. A team then pulled a load of 15 to 20 cakes to shore.

The old ice shed could hold 10,000 cakes. They were slid off the sleigh with chutes that made stacking easier. The ice was stored 12 layers high with sawdust between each layer. Six inches of sawdust was packed around the cakes to insulate the ice through summer.

Grandma Fed Hungry Crew

On a good day, 1,000 cakes could be loaded by three teams of horses and 10 hardy men. Grandma Alfonse would prepare a real lumberman's dinner for the men at noon on days of the harvest.

Grandpa's ice deliveries would begin on April 15 of each year. Home ice delivery came four times a week, more often during extremely hot weather.

Home iceboxes were simple. A draw pan under the box had to be emptied each day. A regular icebox was filled for $2 a month. Businesses bought their ice 200 pounds at a time.

At that time, there were three hotels in town, three meat markets, a hospital, a creamery, restaurants, taverns and a fox farm. All needed ice.

In summers, Grandpa started his days at 5 a.m. He uncovered the ice, washed and loaded it. After a quick breakfast, he started his route. Most days the home deliveries were handled by 1 p.m. Then he delivered large loads to the businesses.

Delivery was done by horse-drawn wagon until 1922, when Grandpa purchased a new Republic truck. The beautiful yellow machine with hard rubber tires was the pride and joy of the whole family. It took family and friends to the county fair in Rice Lake, a long bumpy ride enjoyed by all.

By the 1930s, electric refrigeration was becoming common, and the days of the icebox were numbered. In the early 1940s, a small pickup truck was all Grandpa Alfonse needed to make his deliveries. In 1944, he retired from the business.

Today, my parents, Bob and Carol Sirianni, live in the home Great-Grandpa Alfonse built on the shore of Beaver Dam Lake.

Many in town still recall stopping there during summer for ice. And they warmly recall the good-natured iceman and his gentle horse, who worked through the coldest days of winter—and the hottest days of summer—in Cumberland, Wisconsin.

Photos: Mike Roemer

THE POLAR PLUNGE. These splashers are participating in the annual dip into Lake Michigan on New Year's Day in Door County. It's a cool way to say, "I did it!"

THE AMERICAN BIRKEBEINER is North America's largest cross-country ski marathon. These skiers take on the rolling hills at the start of the race in Cable. The first race took place in 1973.

BORDER PATROL? Susie and Mike Keintz, on a Ski-Doo Renegade 800 E-Tec, ride trails at Land O' Lakes, "the top of Wisconsin".

Far-North Snowmobiling Is Borderline Fun

By Mike Keintz, Land O' Lakes, Wisconsin

THESE DAYS, snowmobiling is a pretty comfortable sport.

Advanced suspensions on machines have eliminated bone-jarring bumps. Heated seats plus hand and foot warmers add greatly to the comfort.

Things were different when I started riding in the early 1960s. Machines then rode rough and were unreliable—you'd ride 'em a few hours, then work on 'em for a week.

My dad ran the Chevy dealership in Benson, Minnesota, and when Johnson Outboards introduced their Skee-Horse snowmobile, he took on the line. There were no trails then, so we rode after school in farm fields and on gravel roads wearing our ice-fishing gear.

In the late '60s, I went to Mankato State University, where I met my wife, Susie. She enjoyed snowmobiling on her parents' farm in Algona, Iowa, where she rode a sled made by Herter's, the sporting goods company best known for duck decoys. More than 100 manufacturers began producing machines in this era.

When I visited the farm, I tried that Herter's sled. It had a ride that hammered your back, and its 440 engine would carry you 70 miles an hour…if you could hang on.

"Back then, they called me 'the bumblebee' because I wore a black-and-yellow Ski-Doo snowmobile suit," Susie recalls. "When I rode the Herter's, the exhaust came straight back at me. It made my suit completely black and I smelled like a chain saw."

As the sport advanced, Susie and I became avid snowmobilers. Here in Land O' Lakes, we've been active members of the Frosty Snowmobile Club for years.

In the 1980s and '90s, we took weeklong snowmobiling treks in Canada and the Black Hills of South Dakota. One morning in Ontario, we woke to a temperature of minus 55. The warmest day that week was minus 20.

Here in Land O' Lakes, the weather's more tame. We're located on the border of Wisconsin and Michigan, so we have the best of both worlds for snowmobiling: You can make new friends, yet find solitude, too.

Head south toward Conover, Eagle River and St. Germain, and you'll meet people at fun places to stop. There are mom-and-pop restaurants and taverns that serve good food all day and most of the night.

To the north in Michigan, the trails don't have all these amenities, but they're so scenic and so little used, you're bound to love them.

A ride that combines both of these worlds is a loop along the border from Land O' Lakes to Hurley and back. It's a good 180 miles, so get ready to ride!

From Land O' Lakes, grab a quick breakfast at the Forest Lake Country Store, then head west on Trail Number 6. You're crossing the top of Vilas County here, one of the densest regions of freshwater lakes in the world.

Tall Pines, Pristine Snow

Enjoy the scenery in the boreal forests of Boulder Junction and Presque Isle Townships with tall white pines, soaring bald eagles and clean, pristine snow.

As you head toward Iron County, you'll have many opportunities to stop and stretch your legs or have lunch. In Mercer, Aunt Esther's Attic is a quaint shop where the ladies like to check out resale items with interesting histories.

Next stop is Hurley and lunch at the Liberty Bell Chalet. Here you'll enjoy the best Italian food in the area. A small gift shop offers Italian bakery, cooking oils and specialty sausages.

From Hurley, turn east on Trail Number 2, which runs along Highway 2 in Upper Michigan. The hilly scenery is a treat to enjoy. But if you've lingered long on the ride out, you can make time on this trail because much of it is an old railroad grade—flat and fast.

A sight worth seeing is Bond Falls, north of Watersmeet. When frozen, it looks spectacular. Also along the way, you'll find the Cisco Chain—14 lovely lakes astride the border.

For local color and characters, we visit Roger's Bar at the north end of the chain. Or, for dinner in a rustic Northwoods setting, you can't beat the food and birchbark wallpaper at Bent's Camp on the south end of the chain.

So come visit Land O' Lakes and see why we love it here. We'd enjoy these trails even if we still rode a Herter's sled… well, maybe not. 🐝

ALL IS CALM...in rural Wisconsin. Near Omro, a family went to ladder-high lengths to give this barn some holiday spirit. A fresh snowfall added a touch of its own. (Rob Resnick photo)

Phooey on Those Pretty White Flakes!

Snow loses its luster for diarist whose winter slowly "goes south".

A COUPLE from Wisconsin kept a "diary" for part of the winter and sent small segments of it regularly to close friends in Florida. Here's how it went:

Dec. 1: Joe and Anne, thought you'd like to know that we're staying "home" here in Wisconsin this winter.

As you're well aware, we spent the last five winters near you there in citrus land. But we so missed the seasonal change, the pure white snow cover and the scent of the pine trees that we decided this year we're going to stay in our cozy home here and "enjoy winter".

Dec. 5: We certainly made the right decision! The first flakes fluttered down today. We'd forgotten how beautiful they are.

Dec. 8: More gentle flurries today. Forecast says we may get as much as an inch. We hope so—it will be so pretty to have everything covered with a soft, pure white blanket.

Dec. 10: We got our wish! It snowed 2 inches. It's *beautiful!* Looks just like one of those scenes you see on a Christmas card.

It was the light, powdery type of flakes. I was able to just sweep off the front walk and even the driveway. We are <u>so</u> <u>glad</u> we decided to stay here!

Dec. 13: Just as Thursday's snow had mostly melted away, we got another 3 inches. How fortunate we are! It's all white and beautiful again—it's just *breathtaking*. You don't know what you're missing!

Dec. 15: Oh boy, what a surprise—another 4 inches. I went to Ace Hardware and got a good-sized snow shovel (do you know what they *charge* for those things now?), and after about an hour I got the walk and drive cleared.

Have to admit I'm aching a little, but it's a good "physical ache".

Dec. 16: An even bigger surprise—two big snowfalls back to back! And speaking of "back", mine's getting a real workout.

I even asked Helen to help me. Together, we eventually got it cleared, and it's now piled pretty high on both sides of the drive. Getting surprisingly cold, too.

Dec. 18: This is kinda unbelievable—the snow just doesn't seem to want to stop. Have to admit, it doesn't seem quite as pretty now.

Due to the low temps—only 6 above—it's all ice underneath. Helen slipped and fell; her back is now sorer than mine, so I have to go it alone.

Even worse, just after I finished, the snowplow driver came by and pushed the end of our driveway shut. But…he's doing his job, so I just shoveled it out again, then went in for three thumbs of brandy.

Dec. 19: The snow's finally slowing, but the temperature's dropped even lower. I'd forgotten how cold it gets here this time of year—goes right to the bone. We both went out to buy heavy winter clothing today. Caps with earflaps, mittens, fur-lined boots, the works.

Do you know how much they *charge* for that stuff now? We hadn't bought any of those things for years.

And then to top off the day, while we were gone, that snowplow jerk went by again and closed the driveway, so I had to shovel our way in!

Dec. 21: This is really something; 5 more inches. We were going to shop for a Christmas tree today, but the way it's coming down, I dunno.

Besides, that darned snowplow came by again, so I would have had another 3 feet of the frozen hard stuff to shovel through.

Dec. 22: I had two reasons to dig out today—the tree, and a trip back to Ace to check out a snowblower.

Do you know what they *charge* for those things these days? Man, you used to be able to buy a <u>truck</u> for that kind of money. So forget it, I'll just be a man and get it done with my dang shovel!

Speaking of *trucks*, that son of a gun went by with that big orange plow again and I had to dig my way back in! Five thumbs of brandy this time.

Dec. 23: Oh my heavens—it's snowing

Joe Sibilski

Benny the Barber Sez...

"One good thing about snow—it makes your lawn look as good as your neighbor's."

Dave Coppersleg

some more! How's the weather down there? I hope it's *raining*.

Helen healed enough to help me, and we both slugged away at it for about 2 hours. She has her own shovel now, and we both have enough calluses to prove we know how to use them.

You're not going to believe this—I think that snowplow guy hides down the street and waits for us to finish! We'd no more gotten into the house and shed all those layers of clothes and here he comes again!!!

If I'd been able to get my boots on fast enough, I would have run out there and hit his truck with my shovel! Added more brandy to our shopping list.

Dec. 24: Well, no worry <u>here</u> about a white Christmas! Got another 6 inches, it's 4 below zero, wind is at 48 mph. The snow is falling sideways!

The only one who might be enjoying this is that snowplow idiot who whooshed by again 10 minutes ago. I rushed out the door in my stocking feet, crunched through 2 feet of snow on the front lawn and threw the shovel at his truck!

<u>I've had it!</u> Phooey on the snow! Phooey on the ice! Phooey on the cold! Phooey on Christmas! And phooey on you in your warm, green little Florida abode! Don't write—I don't want to hear how it is there. I'll see you next year—up close. 🧀

Stuck In the Snow? Doc Came up with a Cure

By Margaret Walz, Columbus, Wisconsin

MY HUSBAND, John, is a general surgeon here in Columbus. All he ever wanted to be was a small-town doctor, and he practices just that way—from the heart.

John (pictured at right) won't hesitate to make house calls or visit patients at all hours, and he proved it in a memorable way during the winter of 2009.

A blizzard had struck southern Wisconsin, and John was happy not to be on call. We settled back for a quiet evening on our farm…or so we thought.

An unexpected emergency call soon came, and we learned an ambulance was on its way to the hospital in Columbus. The surgeon on call was snowed in and couldn't reach the hospital from Sun Prairie.

Could John help this patient? He didn't know, but he had to try.

John jumped into his pickup truck and got going…exactly nowhere. His tires were spinning, so with freezing hands, John installed tire chains, then loaded some weight into the truck bed.

He tried again but never made it out of our driveway.

So there sat the country doctor…in the dark…in a swirling storm…5 miles from the hospital, where he was badly needed. What now?

Then John thought of a vehicle that probably *could* make it through the snow —our Ford backhoe! It would be a cold ride, but he had to try.

All Alone Along Highway

As a Vietnam veteran with over 20 years in the Air National Guard, John had loads of winter gear from the military. I think he was wearing all of it as he waddled to the barn to climb aboard that backhoe.

From the open seat atop the machine, John fired it up, then steered it out of the barn. It was slow going on our windswept country roads, but John had Highway 60 to himself; nobody else was crazy enough to try driving that night.

John reached the hospital, parked the backhoe out front, then ran inside to take care of his patient, who would end up being okay. Afterward, John waited around for the roads to be cleared and caught a ride home with a co-worker.

The backhoe sat in front of the hospital for a few days until the weather was tame enough for a trip back during daylight.

He never wanted publicity, but the local paper did a story on John and his nighttime dash down Highway 60 aboard a backhoe. All his life he's been a simple country doctor, doing whatever he can to care for people.

In med school, this surgeon learned how to operate…but he never knew then that one day a necessary skill would be to operate heavy equipment. 🧀

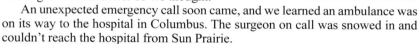

ISLAND SUNRISE. Winter sun over Lake Superior finds Madeline Island dressed in a shimmering cloak of ice. Hard winters are welcome here, as an ice road links the 240-some residents of the island with the mainland at Bayfield. (Nick Bristol photo)

It's All Downhill In Drummond...
And the Locals Love It

Creative sled builders in crazy costumes warm up winter at Bayfield County barstool races.

By Graeme Stewart, Trego, Wisconsin

A HEARTY CHEER goes up from more than 3,000 spectators lining a snow-covered racing slope, as they watch a finely tuned and highly competitive athlete... *topple off a barstool?*

Drummond

It's true...and it's tradition in Bayfield County, where folks travel from all across Wisconsin and beyond to see the Drummond Barstool Races. This fun and frivolity happens on Presidents' Day weekend each year.

"Wipeouts are common, and that's the reason everybody comes," says event founder Craig Manthey.

As president of the Drummond Sno-Jacks Snowmobile Club, he has directed this community fund-raising event since its inception in 1999.

How did a crazy event like a downhill

RIGHT NEAR THE ACTION are the spectators at these races (below). Founder Craig Manthey (at right) watches the competition.

barstool race get started? According to Craig, it began when he attended a meeting of the local snowmobile club, which—like all others in Wisconsin—must raise funds to cover trail-grooming costs.

"We had a chili feed that raised a little each year, and the club really needed new ideas," Craig recalls. "So I said, 'Why don't we do barstool races? All we need is some old barstools...we'll put them on skis and send them downhill.'"

He pauses for effect, then says, "They looked at me like I was nuts."

But not completely, because he'd seen barstool racing draw big crowds when he lived in Montana.

Yes, There Are Rules

The races are run this way: Two-person teams consisting of a rider and a pusher compete. The pushers give the riders a running start, and the riders race downhill, head to head (or stool to stool) against another team. First one to reach the bottom—with his or her bottom still on the stool—wins the race.

The event has become so popular that some 60 competitors fly down a groomed slope maintained with modern snow-making equipment. It's become so sophisticated that the racers are timed by a computer system...a far cry from the first race, as Craig remembers.

"About 20 of us knocked together some sleds and slid them down a ditch bank on Highway N, across the road from the Chequamegon Saloon."

Turned out that raised more money than the chili feed ever did...and was a lot more fun.

So much fun, in fact, that the barstool races have gained national attention for tiny Drummond, population 150. The event has been covered by CNN and was featured on the Discovery Channel's *Wreckreation Nation*, which celebrates wacky sports. This one certainly qualifies.

Picture Elvis piloting a pink Cadillac downhill against a fur-clad trapper on a dogsled. If you find that hard to envision, you can watch the video of it—and more—

"We've sent a pinball machine downhill..."

This event has brought a great deal of exposure and people to this crossroads community, consisting of three bars, one sports shop, a post office and a school. Over $10,000 is raised each year for community causes, with funds going toward school programs and the Bayfield County Alliance, which grooms snowmobile trails countywide.

Town's Claim to Fame

The whole town gets behind the event. Main Street is closed off, sheriff's deputies direct traffic, and shuttle buses ferry spectators from the school parking lot to the hill…all in a town that's three blocks long.

Yes, this is barstool racing, but the gathering is not what the name might imply.

"It's a family event with a warming tent and hot chocolate and hot dogs, chili and more," says Craig. "This isn't about a lot of beer drinking. You couldn't do that if you wanted to, because it's usually so cold on Presidents' Day weekend, a beer would freeze in your hand!

"What else is there to do in Drummond in the middle of winter?" Craig jokes. With this event, the answer is, "A lot."

These barstool races have become this town's claim to fame, and that's fine with the folks here.

on YouTube *(youtube.com/watch?v=_uM hfG8b2eg)*.

"That's in our Open Class, where creativity counts," Craig explains. "Anything you can put on skis is allowed. We've sent a pinball machine downhill, as well as an elaborate-looking battle tank, a bus, a rocket, a deer pulling a sled…. The outfits the riders come up with are hilarious."

While anything goes in the Open Class, some seriously competitive racing happens in the Regular Class, where one team from Menomonie reportedly obtained some Olympic racing skis to outfit their sled. Then there's a Powder Puff division, in which the ladies compete.

Eliason's Motor Toboggan Tamed Winter Trails

Eliason Snowmobiles

SNOWMOBILE INVENTOR Carl Eliason at left with motor toboggan in 1939. At right, 1950s brochures sold these models built in Clintonville.

A bad foot and a passion for the outdoors led to one of Wisconsin's most novel inventions.

By Mike Martin, La Crosse, Wisconsin

BACK IN 1924, it was mighty tough to get around northern Wisconsin during winter.

Although it was the age of the Model T, those vehicles weren't much good on snowy roads, and traveling off road with them was unthinkable. That led a host of amateur inventors to try and come up with some sort of motorized vehicle that could cope with snow and ice.

One of those inventors was a young outdoorsman from Sayner named Carl Eliason. Born in 1899, Carl ran his trapline all winter, even though a crippled foot made it difficult for him to get around.

That lack of mobility led Carl to tinker with a machine that could travel in snow. At first, he "fooled around" with a Model T equipped with skis. But even with skis attached, a large Tin Lizzie was no match for deep snows and unplowed roads.

By winter of 1924, Carl turned his attention to motorizing a smaller type vehicle he was certain could travel over snow —in effect, a motorized toboggan. He worked on the invention in the garage behind his home, traveling frequently to Milwaukee by train to pick up machine parts.

After more than 2 years of tinkering, Carl created his first over-the-snow machine. It was powered by a 2½-horsepower Johnson outboard boat motor that was liquid cooled.

The engine was mounted on the front of a toboggan, and it drove an endless, cleated track. The driver sat in back and steered a pair of skis up front by pulling on ropes.

It was a clever design that worked. Although the engine on Carl's machine would eventually migrate to the back of the toboggan, many of his early power-up-front design principles are present in today's snowmobiles.

Carl was granted a patent on his "motor toboggan" in 1927, but he was probably just as delighted with the mobility it provided.

"With this machine," he later wrote, "I was able to turn the tables on my hunting comrades as long as there was snow on the ground. While they hoofed it on foot, I would ride and get to our destination in the woods an hour ahead of them!"

Each Machine Custom-Built

From 1924 until the beginning of World War II, Carl built approximately 40 more motor toboggans, selling them to hunters, utility workers and outdoorsmen. Since each was custom built, few were exactly alike (some seated four people).

Eventually, Carl switched to motorcycle engines. He was partial to Excelsior and Indian motorcycles because their engines and transmissions were a single unit.

Folks around Sayner could see the value of Carl's invention, but it was slow to catch on elsewhere. Part of that was undoubtedly the cost—$350 to $550—a

ROOM FOR FOUR. Eliasons in this 1928 photo include driver Carl. On back is his father, John, and third is brother Oscar. Second man is James Ovans. In photo at right, Carl drives a '53 model.

considerable sum during the 1920s and the Depression that followed.

Just before World War II, Finland approached Carl about buying a couple hundred machines. Realizing he could never produce that many, Carl negotiated with the Four Wheel Drive Auto Company (FWD) in Clintonville to take over production, with Carl as a consultant.

Although the Finnish deal fell through, the U.S. Army did buy 150 machines to use in Alaska. Between 1940 and 1947, FWD built and sold about 200 of these motorized toboggans.

In 1947, production was moved to another plant in Kitchener, Ontario, where the first rear-engine model was built in 1950. By the mid-1960s, Polaris snowmobiles of Minnesota had taken over the market by incorporating many of Carl's design principles—his original patents had expired by then. The last Eliason Motor Toboggan rolled off a Canadian production line in 1964.

Carl Eliason lived until 1979. He was inducted posthumously into the Snowmobile Hall of Fame in 1991—an honor he never imagined 70 years earlier...when he was a young man who simply needed a better way to get around in the woods. 🛷

The Snowmobile Hall of Fame and Museum is open year-round in St. Germain. Vintage machines include an Eliason Motor Toboggan. For more information, check out *snowmobilehalloffame.com*.

Noteworthy Quotes From Noteworthy Wisconsinites

"IF you'll not settle for anything less than your best, you will be amazed at what you can accomplish in your life."
—*Vince Lombardi*

"THERE are people who make things happen, there are people who watch things happen and there are people who wonder what happened. To be successful, you need to be the person who makes things happen."
—*Jim Lovell, Apollo 13 astronaut, graduate of University of Wisconsin-Madison*

"THE MIDWEST has a certain sense of decency that I don't feel in other places. Maybe I live in a fantasy world, but it seems to me that Midwesterners are a cut above everyone else." —*Greta Van Susteren, TV commentator born in Appleton*

"THE LONGER I live, the more beautiful life becomes. If you foolishly ignore beauty, you will soon find yourself without it."
—*Frank Lloyd Wright, born in Richland Center*

"THEY SAID I was such a great prospect that they were sending me to a winter league to sharpen up. When I stepped off the plane, I was in Greenland."
—*Bob Uecker*

"ONCE Miles Davis asked me, 'What's your secret, Les? People love you.' I said, 'The secret is, I don't play for myself, I play for people. I do my best to entertain.'"
—*Les Paul, born in Waukesha*

"I LIVE every day as if it were Saturday night." —*Al McGuire*

"ALL LOVE that has not friendship as its base, is like a mansion built on sand."
—*Ella Wheeler Wilcox, author and poet, born in Janesville*

"THIS MUG of mine is as plain as a barn door. Why do people pay thirty-five cents to look at it?" —*Spencer Tracy, actor, born in Milwaukee*

"IF YOU WORK harder than somebody else, chances are you'll beat him even though he has more talent than you." —*Bart Starr*

"PEOPLE need a time to laugh. It's up to us comedians to bonk ourselves on the head or slip on a banana peel so the average guy can say, 'I may be bad, honey, but I'm not as much of an idiot as that guy on the screen!'"
—*Chris Farley, born in Madison*

"TIME is the coin of your life. Spend it yourself. Don't allow others to spend it for you." —*Carl Sandburg, political writer, born in Milwaukee*

"HOME is simply the nicest word there is."
—*Laura Ingalls Wilder, author of Little House on the Prairie, born in Pepin*

"IF YOU want a happy ending, that depends, of course, on where you stop your story." —*Orson Welles, born in Kenosha*

"IN every aspect of life, have a game plan, and then do your best to achieve it."
—*Alan Kulwicki, NASCAR driver, born in Greenfield*

"I WAS BORN and raised in Houston, Texas, but Wisconsin is always going to be home for me. I'll always be back." —*Donald Driver*

window on WISCONSIN

Favorite photos shared by readers.

Mighty (Tired) Hunters

Their get-up-and-go got up and left! Longtime deer-hunting pals Nick Hall (left) of Oregon, Wis. and George Grantin of Menasha called it a night early, after a long day in the woods. Photo was taken at their friend John Kobinsky's hunting camp in Fence and shared by Ruth Kobinsky.

Dog Gone Crazy

Mollie the German shorthaired pointer frolicked in the Wisconsin winter snow, "bat ears" and all. Brook Burling of Wisconsin Rapids reports he enjoyed taking this photo of his pet and shares it here.

A New Winter Coat

"One of best things about Wisconsin's winters is that every morning is a surprise," writes Terry McNeill of Dodgeville. Terry captured this tranquil scene not far from his home.

Shots to Share? If you have a photo that captures the beauty of Wisconsin or the fun in living here, send it to: *Our Wisconsin*, 399 S. Hwy. 51, Manitowish Waters WI 54545. Or e-mail to: *editors@OurWisconsinMag.com* and put "Window on Wisconsin" in the subject line.

"Look at This One!"

"This was our first time heading out to cut our Christmas tree as a family," says Kelly Quade of Fredonia. Daughters Savannah, 4, and Caroline, 2, browsed at Greenview Tree Farm in Random Lake, and Kelly says the girls loved searching for that perfect tree.

Ringing Up Ringers

Jim Cook pitches as his friend Jim Hyatt awaits his turn at the annual Winter Horseshoes Extravaganza in Wild Rose. Son Tony Cook writes, "We have a small game feed, a bonfire to stay warm and a cocktail to help our aim."

Collegiate Snow Angel

Zach Proeber, 21, was so happy with a light dusting of snow in Muskego that he had to make a snow angel. Mom Lynn says, "I have to admit I still make them, too. We love our snow…it's Wisconsin, ya know!"

All Aboard!

"The Santa Train visits our town at Christmastime, and my husband, Randy, and I (center) enjoy the ride," relates Linda Johnson of Plymouth. Steam Engine 1003 is part of the Wisconsin & Southern Railroad.

GOING TO THE CHAPEL. Charming wedding chapel in the woods harkens back to days of the past, when horses knew the way to Grandma's house. It's south of Waupaca, on the Crystal River. (Dawn Richards photo)

'It Takes Longer to Milk, and Do Nearly Everything, in Deeply Cold Weather'

Welcome to a week in life of an Amish family...with no car and no electricity.

WE'RE GLAD to see you back at the Yoder farm for another visit!

I'm Owen Yoder, writing this weeklong diary describing life on our farm in northeastern Wisconsin. This is a family operation where everybody pitches in ...even with this diary.

Cecil

We're located on State Highway 117 between Bonduel and Cecil, about 2 miles south of Shawano Lake, where we love to go ice fishing.

Our bakery is open from mid-April to Christmas, and as I write this, we're open just two more weekends this year. We're ready for a break and are counting down the weekends.

We farm 200 acres of organic hay, oats and corn, with pasture for our dairy herd. We're milking 12 heifers, and four more will freshen soon.

My wife, Treva Sue, and I are blessed with nine children. Three daughters are married and so are three sons. At home are three daughters, Katie Mae, Elnora and Carolyn. We finished picking our corn last week and are thankful for a bountiful crop!

Sunday, Dec. 8: At 5 a.m., I stepped outside into snow flurries and zero degrees...feels like more snow is on the way.

It's much nicer inside the barn at 45 degrees. I did the milking and son Steven

---

"Grandsons rode home with Steven—his horse is faster than Grandpa's..."

---

fed the cows and horses. Carolyn came to help because we want to attend church services.

It takes longer to milk—and do just about everything—in deeply cold weather. We have three Jersey-cross calves on the bottle right now and they're frisky! We give them 1-1/2 bottles of milk twice a day on cold days. The chores are soon finished and Diamond, our buggy horse, is enjoying his oats and hay. He's fueling up for a good run this morning.

As we head to the house for a hot breakfast, we meet five of our grandchildren. They're coming to stay with us for a couple days, as their parents will soon leave to attend a funeral in Indiana.

We have plenty of entertainment at the breakfast table with our meal of eggs, bacon and coffee. We leave at 8 a.m. for a 7-mile drive to church.

Diamond pulls a full buggy this morning with the five children aboard. Having so many packed inside makes it toasty warm the whole trip.

We had a visiting minister from Iowa today and heard an interesting sermon on the spiritual ways of life we need to follow. Afterward, we enjoyed a light lunch and some visiting.

When we prepared to head for home, grandsons Steven Dale, Anthony and Luke Devon said they'd rather ride home with Uncle Steven...because his horse goes faster than Grandpa's! They'd mentioned this matter on the way to church.

Granddaughters Anna Mae and Tina Rose rode with us, though, and when we arrived home the first thing I did was check on the heifers and push up some feed, then get Diamond fed.

Now we can act lazy for a couple hours. Treva made cashew crunch popcorn, my favorite treat at this time of year. When Steven and Roseanna showed up with the three boys, they couldn't wait to tell me how much fun it was to pass us on the way home from church!

Steven and I did chores and made sure everything was closed up for the cold night ahead, then took for the warm house and a hot supper of chunky beef soup and sandwiches.

After supper, the boys had books to look at and some games to play. Soon it was time to slip under the covers for a good night's sleep.

Monday, Dec. 9: What a cold morn-

Photos: Bob Firth

FOR RELIGIOUS REASONS, Amish adults avoid close-up photos of themselves. Instead of picturing our diarist or his family, we're showing scenes of Wisconsin's peaceful Amish country.

ing it is to get everything moving—including me. It's zero again with the wind blowing and snow in the air. The cows had good appetites this morning.

Steven jumped on his bike for the short ride home and I headed into the house, where the grandchildren are ready for Grandma's breakfast. We enjoyed fried eggs, taters and tomato gravy. After breakfast, we had devotions.

Treva and the girls have some candy to make to fill orders, so they'll work on that most of the day while caring for the grandchildren.

I did bookwork in the morning while Steven put out bales for the horses and heifers, then finished up the other chores.

We warm up with a light lunch, but much as I'd like, I don't have time for a nap. A local taxi driver, Mary Mueller, took me to town for supplies. I picked up 12 rubber mats to put in the tie stalls for our heifers.

Around noon, did the wind ever start to blow! We installed four mats, then milked, fed and bedded down the cows with fluffy chopped straw. We hope the barn stays warm enough with only half our stalls full.

On cold evenings like this, right near the coal stove is my favorite spot.

Tuesday, Dec. 10: At 5 a.m., it's 5 below zero, windy and snowing as I briskly walked to the barn.

I'm glad it feels warm inside…at least compared with outside. We had to jump-

---

> *"We heard an interesting sermon on the spiritual life we should lead…"*

---

start the diesel generator to power our milking equipment; I later found a bad battery connection. We have no electricity in our home, but we do use a generator for our business. The cows will stay inside today for their feedings.

We had a delicious breakfast for a cold morning—fried corn mush, liverwurst, homemade apple butter and tomato gravy.

At 8, Harold Otto, our taxi driver, picked us up to go to Clintonville for some Christmas shopping. Steven and Roseanna joined us, as well as our daughter Leona and her children. It turned out to be a nice sunny day, but again very cold.

We returned home at 3 o'clock to a warm house. Treva and the girls had to get a candy order done this evening. Son La Mar, wife Linda Fern and their children gave a helping hand filling the candy order while Steven and I did the chores.

When chores were finished, supper was waiting—fried chicken, burgers and soup. LaMar's family had supper with us.

Wednesday, Dec. 11: The cows turn their heads my way looking for a bite of some hay…that's the way they and we start our mornings.

It's zero yet again, but the diesel fires up the way it should, and that brings me a sigh of relief.

Today the candy making continues.

DOWN A COUNTRY ROAD. Amish buggies are a common sight in the ridge lands near the village of Westby in Vernon County.

CORN SHOCKS stand to dry in the snowy stubble fields near Westby, southeast of La Crosse. Amish settlers came to Westby in 1966. Barn raising (right) blends old-time construction techniques with modern materials.

We'll also ship out some fruitcakes. Elnora was at her teaching job, which she does 3 days a week; she'll be home the rest of the week to help in the bakery.

I had a pile of bookwork waiting on me, so I worked on that 'til noon. Steven took care of chores in the barn, keeping feed in front of the cows. He joined us for lunch, as his wife, Roseanna, was visiting her folks for the day.

We had ham and cheese sandwiches and some soup. Oh, what a good day to sneak in a snooze beside the stove!

This afternoon we installed more rubber mats for the heifers. After chores, we had a snack and relaxed in the living room until bedtime.

Thursday, Dec. 12: We're up at 4 a.m. to start baking, and I begin by adding coal to the stove. It's minus 2 outside.

I started the diesel generator to turn on the lights and warm up the room for the bakers. I stopped in the barn to make sure no heifers were freshening, then returned to the house until milking time at 5:30.

It's my morning to make breakfast, as everybody's busy in the bakery. I fried up a pan of bacon and brewed a pot of fresh coffee. We have plenty of warm cookies coming out of the oven, too.

Steven and I chopped some bedding for the heifers. We had to adjust the chopper, which was plugging up. It seems in the winter, chores never get done smoothly through the day.

Treva, Katie and I went to Shawano for some business after lunch. I also stopped at Lawrenz's Sausage Shop in Bonduel for some good snack sticks and other home-made sausages. It's owned by a local family —do try it if you happen to be passing through Bonduel.

The girls are working hard today because they want to leave for their first ice-skating of the season, an evening they enjoy with other young folks. They hitched up May, the Morgan mare, to the buggy and took the 4-mile ride to the Edward Schrocks' pond.

Treva and I spent a quiet evening writing letters and reading. When I went to the barn to sweep up feed and turn out the lights, guess what I found? A heifer in the freshening pen with a nice heifer calf! She was taking good care of her newborn.

We always give heifers warm water after freshening, and she downed two 5-gallon pails of water and ate a slice of dry hay after licking her calf dry. That's a good indicator she's on her way to filling the milk bucket soon.

After I made sure that she and the little one were all right, it was midnight when I walked into the quiet house. All too soon, it would be time to bake.

Friday, Dec. 13: We got busy in the bakery at 4 a.m. I made a run to the barn to check on the new calf and found everything was fine.

We did our normal routine…I mixed the bread and Treva prepared the coffee cakes. The girls then baked the bread and packaged the cookies.

We're short of help because Elnora has to go back to her teaching job. Nelda Yoder, the regular teacher, broke her elbow while ice-skating.

Steven and I did the chores. The new heifer is very quiet and easy to milk; her calf took two bottles of colostrum.

After we finished and had our breakfast, Steven checked the water tanks for the horses and heifers. This time of year we have to chop ice so they can get at the water.

I waited on bakery customers in the afternoon—this close to our annual closing, people stock up on our baked goods to freeze—and it was a steady flow of business. The girls took over early so I could do chores; we want to attend a birthday surprise party for a neighbor tonight.

We finished chores at 6:15, then noticed a heifer in the freshening pen needs attention. Another heifer calf was born! We got a chunk of dry hay and 10 gallons

> *"Bakery customers stock up on goods to freeze at the end of the year…"*

of warm water for her…and we'll check on her first thing when we get home.

Back from the birthday party at 10 p.m., and wow, is it cold! I put Diamond in the barn with feed and water for the night, then checked the heifer. Her calf is dry, and everybody is calmed down in dry fluffy straw. I grabbed a bag of coal for the stove and headed for the house.

We're thankful for our warm home tonight, and I have to wonder about all the homeless people and hope they have a place to be warm. We count our blessings as we get under the covers.

Saturday, Dec. 14: Treva and I get everything going in the bakery, and as I leave to milk, the girls say, "Happy birthday, Dad!"

Yes, it's my 56th…where has the time gone?

The first thing I see in the barn is the baby calf, contentedly suckling at its mother. Its little tail is really wiggling…*what a miracle.*

The chores go great, and even milking the heifer is easy; she never even raises a foot. We're down to two heifers to freshen.

At 8 a.m., the girls opened the bakery and customers came steadily, but it slowed by afternoon.

So ends another busy week and a good visit with friends at *Our Wisconsin*. The Yoder family wishes everyone a blessed New Year. 🧀

DOG TALES WORTH TELLING 🐾

WHETHER they're farm dogs, hunting dogs or house pets, the remarkable sixth sense of these lovable companions is often uncanny.

Our Wisconsin readers have shared some fascinating dog tales in the past year. Here are just a few you'll find interesting:

"Our boys had a paper route when they were young. One morning they were both so ill, they told my husband he'd have to deliver the papers.

"He said, 'Okay, where's the list?'

" 'There is no list,' the boys replied. 'Just take the dog.'

"Turned out this 'paper pooch' would go to each porch where the paper was to be dropped, then head to the next stop.

"And no one called to complain abouat not getting the paper!"

Here's another reader memory:

"One spring day we couldn't find Sparky. After calling him again and again, we spotted him way out in a newly planted cornfield.

"It appeared he was playing with some white object, which we thought was a milk jug. We called him again, but he didn't move. So we assumed he'd come home when he got hungry.

"The better part of the afternoon passed, and Sparky remained in the field. So my husband decided to investigate.

"He found Sparky holding down our daughter's pet white rabbit with his paws. The rabbit had escaped its cage, and in all of the busyness of the day, we hadn't missed it.

"When my husband arrived, Sparky gave him a look that seemed to say, 'What took you so long?' "

And here's another dog tale:

"When I was growing up, our family moved from a farm 2 miles north of town to one 2 miles south of town. For several weeks after that move, Brownie, our German shepherd, would be lying wet and tired by the porch most mornings.

"We didn't know why 'til the farmer who took over our place met my dad in town one day and said, 'I don't see you much, but I see your dog a lot. Appears he's digging up his old bones and hauling them home.'

"That's a true story. Now, mind you, Brownie had ridden to our new place in the cab of a truck. So how could he have possibly known his way to that farm and back, 4 miles away?"

The sixth sense of dogs is amazing!

ONLY GUS KNOWS. This inquisitive springer, Gus, checks out a winter visitor he met in Egg Harbor. (Melody Carranza photo)

Still Dukin' It Out at 75!

This Milwaukee attorney laces up the gloves and climbs through the ropes to regularly compete in a Masters boxing league.

By Roy Reiman

BY DAY, Mike Tarnoff jabs at opponents in court. By night, he's pummeling a bag in his basement. And on other occasions he's in the ring, punching a puffing opponent about the same age.

Mike has duked it out in 26 matches over the past 10 years—in Milwaukee, Chicago, New York, Kansas City and London —and has won about two-thirds of them. As this is written, he's preparing for yet another bout…and really looking forward to it.

"I do this for the fun of it," he says. "I'm not planning to turn pro anytime soon!"

Who knew men in their 60s and 70s were still boxing? We certainly didn't. But we've learned over 100 seasoned warriors —Mike among them—compete in "Masters" matches (think Seniors or Masters in golf) at an event in Kansas City each fall.

They come from all walks of life, but likely few are lawyers of Mike's caliber. He's practiced law in Milwaukee for over 50 years and is past president of the

LAW-ABIDING BOXER. Mike Tarnoff waits in corner before donning headgear for a recent match. In the photo at top, he's punching away in one of 26 bouts across the country.

Wisconsin Academy of Trial Lawyers.

So why would a 75-year-old suit-and-tie guy want to climb through the ropes and mix it up with people who are eager to trade punches? We asked.

Isn't this a little risky, boxing in your 70s?

There are some people who think that. But I've played sports all my life, and you reach an age when you can't play basketball or football anymore…I missed the competition.

Then I read an article about some older boxers competing in what they call "white-collar boxing" at Gleason's Gym in Brooklyn, and learned there were a number of other ring events around the country. I boxed in my 20s and hadn't fought for years, so I decided to make a comeback.

After getting in shape, I went to a national tournament in Kansas City where there were five guys my age and weight. One fighter was 78, and he fared fine.

It's not as dangerous as most people think. We wear headgear and use 16-ounce gloves. In my view, bicycling is more dangerous—almost everyone who rides a bike, including me, has been in an accident of some kind. I've had 14 surgeries over the years—knees, wrists, rotator cuffs and more. None came from boxing. So I'm

PREPARING FOR BATTLE. Mike relaxes before a bout, thinking through his approach in the fight just ahead. His wife, Carol, lends a supporting hand; he contends she's not concerned.

never scared when I step in the ring. After 26 matches, the worst I've suffered is a broken nose, and that was my fault.

Does your wife attend your bouts? Does she get concerned?

She was concerned early on, but not much anymore. I tell her it's like any other sport—you have to fight smart. You need to keep your head down, protect your jaw, study your opponent, stay alert.

In one of my earlier matches in Chicago, I boxed really dumb. The guy got the decision, and when I watched the tape later, I saw why he deserved to win.

At a rematch 6 months later, I beat him pretty handily. In fact, he took a standing eight-count in the third round.

How long are these matches?

They're three 2-minute rounds. When I tell friends that, some say, "Oh, is that all?" And I tell them, "You try it sometime! You'll see how long 2 minutes can be when it's that intense."

You said you boxed when you were younger. Where?

I boxed at the University of Wisconsin and at Marquette University. I was never good enough to be the No. 1 guy in my weight class at UW.

Boxing was a huge Big Ten sport from the 1930s through 1960…up to 15,000 people attended the national tournaments at the Field House in Madison. UW boxers won eight NCAA team titles.

There were maybe 50 guys on the team, but only seven or eight competed in matches with other schools.

Wasn't boxing dropped at UW because a fighter died after a match?

Yes, that was in 1960—the year I graduated—and it was a guy on our team at the NCAA finals. In fact, I was at that match.

His name was Charlie Mohr. He was fast and moved a lot, so most guys couldn't hit him. They tried to get inside and slug with him. He wasn't real strong as boxers go. He looked like a professor and acted like one—a smart boxer.

He was boxing Stu Bartell, from San Jose State, whom he'd beaten before. But when Bartell got inside, he caught Charlie with a single right to the head and he went down. It didn't look like he got hurt that bad, but he later collapsed and died a week later from brain damage.

There was a big uproar on both sides, but that ended college boxing.

How did you originally get into boxing?

When I was real young I used to watch *Friday Night Fights* with my dad. And he sometimes took me to matches…maybe I was trying to show people how tough I was. (Laughs.)

What I like about boxing is the aspect of self-reliance. You're in the ring alone with no teammates to cover for you or help. It's all on you.

In a way it's like a jury trial. In there you're alone, too. If you want to succeed, you have to keep fighting back. You have to be resourceful. Just like in boxing, you're looking for any weakness and capitalize on it when you find it.

So you're 75, with all these surgeries, and plan to keep on boxing. How does your doctor feel about that?

Hey, if anything, he encourages me. I had open-heart surgery with a bypass 4 years ago, and my doc says to keep on fighting as long as I stay in shape.

And I do work on that. I'm already spending 30 minutes or more daily getting ready for my next match. I'm looking forward to it!

Boxing Packed Punch in Wisconsin

COLLEGE BOXING was a huge sport from the 1930s through 1960, and Wisconsin was at the epicenter of it all. Here's evidence from the book *Lords of the Ring* by Doug Moe:

- On the very same night in 1940 when Joe Louis defended his world heavyweight title before 11,000 fans in New York's Madison Square Garden, collegiate boxers battled before 15,000 fans in the UW Field House in Madison.
- The UW Field House was routinely packed with over 10,000 fans for NCAA boxing tournaments. Folding chairs were put on the basketball court to jam in 15,000. And one-third of those crowds were women.
- Many elite athletes—who later became famous—boxed in the Field House during this era. Among them were Olympic prospects including Cassius Clay (later Muhammad Ali).
- There appeared to be a special bond among athletes who faced each other in the ring. Athletic Director Elroy Hirsch once said that no athletes at UW stayed closer over the years than Badger boxers. Even today they loyally return for reunions.
- Mike Tarnoff says the same is true among senior boxers he faces. "We get together before and after matches, and have great respect for each other. They're good guys and have become good friends."

White Deer Roam in Their Backyard

*These "ghosts of the forest" fascinated wildlife watchers for centuries—
and add much to the lives of these fortunate neighbors.*

LIFE IN THE NORTHWOODS. Marshia and Mike Crowley enjoy all the wildlife around them.

THEY MIX. White deer in this local herd live, feed and breed with regularly colored deer.

A COLORFUL FAMILY. White does give birth to offspring that are either brown or white.

A WHITE FAWN is produced when both parents carry a rare recessive gene for albinism.

By Mike and Marshia Crowley
Boulder Junction, Wisconsin

Boulder
Junction

WE LIVE in far northern Wisconsin and feel lucky to reside in this dense forest surrounded by hundreds of lakes.

We're luckier still to live with the abundant wildlife here, and like all of our neighbors, we're in awe every day of our local herd of "ghost deer"—a rare population of white deer that lives in this portion of Vilas County.

They received attention in recent years with the 2007 publication of Jeff Richter's splendid book *White Deer: Ghosts of the Forest*. Then, in 2009, when a documentary aired on Wisconsin Public Television went viral online, it gave a national audience of more than a million people a glimpse into the world of white deer.

This makes us all the more privileged to live near these rare creatures...they're often right outside our home. No matter how many times we see them, it's a treat.

Predate America's Settlement

This white deer population is thought to have been here for centuries. Naturalist John Bates of Manitowish traces historic references of them to North America's settlement. European explorers named many of the major lakes in the vicinity, and there's evidence in the literature of at least one: White Deer Lake, in nearby Forest County.

The white deer also play an important role in the creation stories of Native American people, such as the Chippewa, who live here. Handed down through the ages, these legends long predate white settlers.

We lived in Montgomery, Illinois and vacationed for 15 years in and around Boulder Junction. When we retired here in 1998, the Northwoods appealed to us for many reasons, beginning with Mike's penchant for musky fishing.

But the white deer were another reason. It's not far-fetched to say they played a part in our decision to spend our retirement years in Boulder Junction.

Mike's long interest in photography came into full bloom, and he bought more equipment. He plowed up a meadow on our property and established a wildlife food plot.

Eventually, we had a family of albino deer coming regularly. They're wild and wary, but Mike has found ways to stay hidden and photograph them from a distance.

According to naturalist Bates, it's unknown if these deer are true albinos or if they're colored white for some other biological reason. Mammologists estimate

one fawn in 10,000 will be born albino.

Albinism happens when both parents carry a recessive gene, Bates explains, so that makes the odds long indeed that an albino birth will occur. Such births obviously occur more regularly than usual near Boulder Junction.

The numbers of white deer in our neighborhood seem to have declined in the last few years, yet we've heard of white fawns being born within a few miles of here.

No Studies Undertaken

The condition of this herd and its dynamics remain open to speculation because no scientific study has been done.

"The white deer are interesting, and I've seen them through the years," says Wisconsin DNR deer researcher Keith McCaffery. "All white deer are protected in Wisconsin for their novelty, and the DNR's emphasis has been to manage harvestable deer in the greater herd, so that's why no time has gone into studying them."

Albino deer occur in many places in North America, but this local herd is noted as one of the largest. McCaffery says another sizable population has been de-

---

"One fawn in 10,000 will be born albino..."

---

scribed in New York State, but it is within a fenced area tied to a military base. The white deer in Wisconsin roam freely.

We've noticed the albinos and their brown brethren readily intermix. Yet the white deer that visit us can be quite aggressive toward most brown deer and stay in a pretty tight group.

In fact, we have videos of four white does fending off a whole herd of brown deer in competition for food. We also have videos of white does protecting their regular-colored fawns. You can see about two dozen of these clips that we've posted at *youtube.com/mmnorthwoods*.

When they're near food, deer commonly rear up on their hind legs and kick at one another in displays of dominance. This pecking-order behavior is to establish who eats first, and we see it often at our food plot. Even mothers who protected their young early on won't hesitate to take a good kick at them months later when competing to feed.

If you'd like to see more of Mike's best still shots of the white deer in our neighborhood, visit our Web site, *lifeinthenorthwoods.com*. Or, plan a trip to the Boulder Junction area and you may catch a glimpse of them.

Spring's Here...
And It's So Welcome!

When it's finally April, Wisconsinites head outdoors to watch the reawakening. Returning songbirds announce its arrival in southern counties, then take their musical message north.

When spring arrives in Wisconsin, you can hear it as well as see it. Streams and rivers are babbling again. Robins are chirping. Spring peepers are...peeping. And newborn calves are testing their voices on Wisconsin dairy farms.

What was that? *Thunder*? What a welcome rumble. We're all ready for that first gentle shower that will surely bring May flowers.

Seemingly overnight, the whole state changes color...with buds burgeoning on back lawns...tulips and daffodils petaling about...and pastures showing what the color "green" really looks like.

As April arrives, fishing fanatics are already spooling new line for their favorite rods, and likely faking a few casts in the garage.

They're picturing quiet days ahead on a lake smooth as a mirror... below a morning moon reluctantly yielding to the day ahead...when the only sound is the gentle lapping against the side of the boat...until a lone loon warbles a call that touches one's soul.

In a state that has 982,155 acres of water—which represents just 2.6% of the state—there will be plenty of "only in Wisconsin" experiences to enjoy in the flower-filled spring days just ahead.

Jerry Tang

SPRING IS DANDY. During halftime at a soccer game, Kassy Tang, 4, enjoyed the dandelions. Grandpa Jerry snapped her picture.

Eileen Herrling

SPRINGTIME COLOGNE. If you take a deep breath, you can almost pick up the scent of these beautiful crab apple blossoms. Even early corn like that at far right has its own fragrance.

Linda Freshwaters Arndt

SEASONAL COLOR. "I look forward to the spring transformation as male goldfinches' plumage turns from boring olive green to striking gold," says Linda Freshwaters Arndt.

SPRING IN A VASE. The white catkins of the common pussy willow seem to trigger the Wisconsin tradition of clipping a few branches and bringing a little bit of spring indoors to enjoy.

Mike Grandmaison

Jeffrey Phelps

SNUG AND SAFE is a whitetail fawn in the understory of a maple woods near the town of Erin. Fawns rely on their lack of scent and natural camouflage for protection.

Eileen Herring

Linda Freshwaters Arndt

STRUTTING HIS STUFF. Backlit with sunlight, this wild gobbler displays in competition for hens in a field outside Winter. Since its reintroduction by the DNR with 29 birds from Missouri back in 1976, the Eastern Wild Turkey has thrived here.

SOARING COLORS. Whether they're store-bought or homemade, kites offer springtime fun that generations of Wisconsinites have enjoyed. The Wisconsin Kiters Club is a membership organization that hosts kite-building workshops and events, including a November 11 "Veterans Day Honor Fly".

TULIP TIME is in April and May at Boerner Botanical Gardens in Hales Corners. Built by the WPA in the 1930s, Boerner is an internationally known horticultural showplace. Modeled after traditional English country gardens, it contains statuary and walking paths.

IT'S TULIP TIME! This colorful array caught the eye of photographer Ken Dequaine in a country garden near Clintonville.

SPRING'S A KICK! Izzy Kellner and her twin brother, Zach, have a single goal in mind as they play soccer on a warm weekend at Broadview Park in Allouez. Their team, known as the Purple Ninjas, is a member of the Allouez Anchors Youth Soccer Club in this southern suburb of Green Bay.

THE TRUE COLOR OF SPRING in Wisconsin is often robin's egg blue. Our prolific state bird can produce as many as three broods per year, and perhaps 40 percent of their nests will produce young.

EARLY ARRIVAL. The common loon is among the first migratory water birds to return to Wisconsin's lakes at ice out. On arrival, the breeding pairs begin searching for suitable nesting sites. Most loons here nest by mid-May. Chicks can dive and find food on their own at 8 weeks.

JEEPERS PEEPERS. One of the first frogs to emerge and breed after winter, the northern spring peeper inflates a large vocal sac to the size of a 25-cent piece, then expels air to make its signature sound. This peeper was photographed in Trempealeau County.

MARSH MARIGOLDS, or "cowslips", are one of the first wildflowers seen in spring, always in wet areas. This perennial patch was spotted near the village of Gilman.

What You Should Know About BIRDS...

They can't smell, they can't taste...you'll learn much more from Wisconsin's "bird expert".

By Roy Reiman

REALLY? Birds have no sense of smell? If we'd learned that earlier in life, we all could have saved a lot of birds.

Remember? We were always told that if a bird falls out of its nest, there's no use putting it back because once the mother picks up human scent on the little one, she won't care for it.

Now, way too late, we learn from George Harrison—known nationally as one of the leading bird authorities—that Mama can't smell that well. In fact, she can't smell at all.

Springtime makes this a timely subject, when songbirds begin returning to Wisconsin after spending the winter in the South (as though they were seniors). And it will likely be of interest to many readers, because a recent survey showed over 55 million Americans feed wild birds.

So while observing backyard birds may be no more than a hobby for you, for all the companies producing birdseed, birdhouses, feeders and squirrel foilers, it's a song.

Before we get into our interview with George, here's a bit of his background. He grew up in Pennsylvania, where his father was a pioneer in the field of wildlife photography. George was in his footsteps most of his early life.

After earning a degree in journalism from Penn State, George worked at the Virginia Game Commission, then became editor of *Pennsylvania Game News*. Next came his big break.

At 29, he became managing editor of *National Wildlife*. "I needed Dad's help in that role, so he accompanied me on world trips to the Galapagos, South Africa, South America and India," George says. "Turnabout is fair play."

In recent years, he's been a regular columnist for *Birds & Blooms* magazine, has written 11 books and produced five PBS specials about backyard birds. He also spent time in the service, retiring as a Major in the infantry after 13 years, mostly in the Reserves. He lives in Hubertus.

George, how did you gradually zero in on birds and become "Wisconsin's leading bird expert"?

My zeroing in on birds wasn't gradual. My parents tell me when I was in my crib, I loved watching birds at feeders just outside the window. I could identify most common birds and their songs by age 10.

A big turning point for me was when I arranged a feature in *National Wildlife* written by three biologists titled, "Invite Wild-

life to Your Backyard". It became the Federation's most reprinted article, well into the millions.

After noting that interest, I built my career around being an expert on backyard wildlife, especially birds, which eventually led to the books, PBS specials and many other things.

So, is it true that birds can't smell?

Yes, that's true. That's because their olfactory system (sense of smell) is poorly developed. Only seabirds and vultures can smell food. Songbirds find their food by sight.

And it's true birds have no sense of taste as well?

Taste and smell use the same organ, so birds cannot taste food the way we can. While humans have 9,000 taste buds, songbirds have fewer than 50.

I don't advise it, but this is why some people put cayenne pepper in birdseed to discourage squirrels. While the squirrels may go "Yikes!" and avoid such seed, birds will eat it without hesitation. They don't detect the strong scent or taste of the pepper. So birds choose their food primarily by sight and touch, relying on genetic programming to determine what seed is best for them.

How about their hearing—some people contend robins can hear earthworms underground.

That's not true. People see robins cock their heads and think they're listening. No, robins cock their heads so they can see the worms better with one eye.

Can birds detect color?

Birds can see color. In fact, birds have a greater sense of color than we do—they can see ultraviolet. That means a male cardinal doesn't appear to be the same color of red to a female cardinal as the red we see. Unlike people, birds can see both "visual" and UV light, giving them a very different color image.

Speaking of color, why is it that male songbirds are more brightly colored than females?

It's because the female covers the nest during the incubation period, so she needs to be camouflaged. Nature just takes care of things like that.

BIRD TALK. George Harrison enjoys sharing information that leads to a greater appreciation of birds.

"YES, MOM, WE'RE HUNGRY!" The robin is Wisconsin's state bird, and these two little beggars will likely be hunting for worms on their own in a month or so. At left is a brilliant cardinal, one of the few birds with an orange bill, and at lower left is a chickadee, named for its "chick-a-dee-dee" call as it busily flits about feeders.

What kind of seed do you recommend to attract certain desired birds?

I've found the food that attracts most seed-eaters is medium hulled (cracked) sunflower seed. The problem is this food is also the favorite of gray squirrels, and matching wits with them can be a full-time job!

A solution is to use safflower seed, which is not favored by squirrels yet attracts a wide variety of birds. Of course, nyjer (thistle) seed is the favorite of finches.

What kind of feeder is best for beginners?

A hopper feeder is best because it keeps seeds dry, stores seed and allows it to flow as needed. Look for one that has a flat support for perching, because birds such as cardinals prefer a flat surface to stand on while eating rather than a round peg.

Back to hummers—how are they able to "park" in the air as they do?

Hummers can stay stationary in the air and even fly backward because, instead of "flapping" their wings like most birds, they actually "pivot" them back and forth at a blurring pace.

So how come they don't have rotator cuff problems?! Is it true hummers harvest spiderwebs to support the outside of their thimble-size nests?

Yes, it is, and for good reason. Spiderweb is known to be one of the strongest fabrics ever tested. You've likely noted how a single strand is so sturdy that it can last for days in the wind while stretched between two trees.

These little hummers are incredibly smart. They use these spiderwebs while building their nests to make them sturdy, but also so their nests can s-t-r-e-t-c-h when their babies are hatched to

SITTING PRETTY. Hummingbirds can fly forward or backward since they "pivot" their wings. Some strengthen their nests with spiderweb.

allow more space in their living room.

Is it true you have a library of over 80,000 wildlife images?

Yes, that's true, and more than half of them are of birds. Amazingly, I never get tired of photographing or observing birds. There's always something magnetic about how birds behave— watching them eat, fight, court, build nests, lay eggs, raise their young, migrate great distances, etc.—it still excites me.

What is your latest book, and how can readers order it?

My most recent book was *Squirrel Wars,* which shows bird-feeding enthusiasts the best way to deal with these ingenious creatures. It wasn't difficult to fill a book with that!

It's available, along with a few bird books, on my Web site: *thebackyardbirdwatcher.com.*

Thanks, George, for sharing your keen knowledge of wild birds. I think I know what you're going to do now...

Yes, I'm heading to my backyard to feed and watch the birds.

window on WISCONSIN

Favorite photos shared by readers.

Sure Sign of Spring

Commonly seen in March and April, Eastern bluebirds are at a 45-year population high here, thanks in part to nest boxes erected by bird lovers. This is the greatest recovery of a songbird population in our state history. Photo shared by Shawano County Field Editor Jim Leuenberger.

Lena's a Long Way from Baltimore

"We used a ladder to climb up and see an oriole nest in a tree in our yard," writes Martha Rose Weaver from Lena. "Here, our granddaughter Savannah peeps in. Her father, Anthony, counted four fledglings. Later, we heard such a fluttering high overhead; the mother bird was encouraging her young to fly."

Spring Promenade

"Before attending prom, students from Luther High School promenaded through Riverside Park in La Crosse," writes Janet Horstman of Sparta. The high school is located in nearby Onalaska.

Roaring River

"This is the Black River at flood stage," relates Cathy Kruckenberg of Whitehall. "We were camping near Hixton, about 12 miles from Black River Falls, and could hear the sound of the river long before we saw it."

Lovely Lupine

Often seen in meadows and at roadsides, this wildflower can be equally at home in your garden. These colorful blossoms were shot by Shell Foeckler of Superior. In Wisconsin, lupine begins blooming in mid-May. Don't miss Lupine Junefest in Mercer each June.

That's a Whopper!

"Our granddaughter McKayla was pretty proud of this bluegill she caught at Mead Lake in Clark County," write Henry and Lois Aumann of Loyal, who sent the picture. "McKayla loves to fish, and often will be the only person in a fishing party to catch some," they add.

Shots to Share? If you have a photo that captures the beauty of Wisconsin or the fun in living here, send it to: *Our Wisconsin*, 399 S. Hwy. 51, Manitowish Waters WI 54545. Or e-mail to: *editors@OurWisconsinMag.com* and put "Window on Wisconsin" in the subject line.

Capitol Improvement

Spring brings colorful tulip gardens...and this is one we can all be proud of. "Here's our state capitol on a nice spring day," says Edgar Catacutan from Franklin. "Despite tumultuous debates that sometimes occur inside the building, there's beauty on the outside."

He's the Lombardi Of Horse Racing

*When the crowd hears "...And they're off!"
at the Derby, few will be more charged up than
Wisconsin's famed horse trainer.*

By Roy Reiman

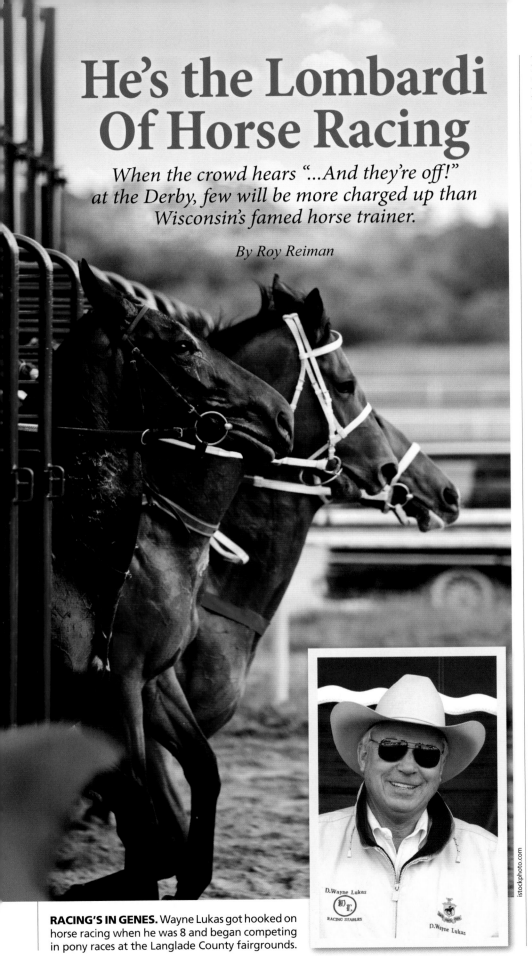

RACING'S IN GENES. Wayne Lukas got hooked on horse racing when he was 8 and began competing in pony races at the Langlade County fairgrounds.

HE'S 78, with the fire and drive of a yearling colt. Respected and feared by his peers on the racing circuit, D. Wayne Lukas is still ready to give anyone a run for his money, any day on any track.

That zest for winning will be on display again this spring, when a national audience hears *"...And they're off!"* at the Kentucky Derby. He's saddled 47 Derby horses to date, and won this "Granddaddy of Derbies" four times. But he's itching for another trip to the winner's circle with the same fervor as the first.

Wayne had several entries in last year's (2014) race, and insiders said his best shot was a leggy horse named Strong Mandate. But the garland of roses didn't end up looped over Mandate's head, and Wayne was already looking toward the next race.

He's horse racing's Lombardi; nothing beats winning.

Over the years, he's won enough trophies to fill a horse trailer. Thoroughbreds he has trained have not only won the

"He grew up with a lot of horse sense..."

Kentucky Derby four times, they've won the Preakness six times, the Belmont four times and the Breeder's Cup 19 times. He's the only trainer ever to win the Triple Crown with two different horses in the same season—one horse won two of the races and the other won the third.

Simply put, D. Wayne Lukas is one of the most successful trainers in the history of Thoroughbred racing. And it all started on a small farm near Antigo.

Caught Horse Fever Early

To say he grew up with a lot of horse sense is an understatement. He began by racing his pony at the Langlade County fairgrounds. By age 8, with some help from his dad, he was already buying, selling and training horses.

Even during high school—where he excelled at basketball—and later during college, he carved out time for horses. Same was true while he worked on his master's in education at UW-Madison and served as a freshman basketball coach under head coach John Erickson.

Wayne says the lessons he learned then —the importance of strong observation skills and the fact that good coaches are good teachers—were invaluable. He uses those same principles when training horses: "It takes a good eye and gut reaction to determine what a horse is capable of doing and what he isn't."

istockphoto.com

After college, he became a high school teacher and a basketball coach at Logan High School in La Crosse for 9 years. He chose those professions because his mother wanted him to make a contribution to society. That background is why he's still known as "The Coach" by friends.

During summer breaks from teaching, Wayne began training horses in South Dakota. By 1967, he was ready to turn to it full-time and began training quarter horses.

He kept learning...and winning. He became so successful that in 1975, his 150 victories doubled the record of the most quarter horse wins in a year by a trainer.

By 1978, he was ready for a new challenge—he switched to training Thoroughbreds. And success came again.

By 1987, he'd set another record—he had 92 stakes winners and became the first trainer to amass more purse earnings than the leading jockey.

Improved with "Seasoning"

And now, at 78, he's not slowing down. In fact, he sees his years as an advantage.

"There's no how-to book in Thoroughbred racing," he says. "Experience is paramount. The trial and error in making mistakes, correcting them, observing these horses on a daily basis—it's a constant learning process."

For that reason, he continues to follow the same rigorous schedule he has for years. "I've always believed if you are going to achieve anything, you need to get up and get going.

"So I wake up every morning at 3:30—no matter where I am in the country, no matter what time zone. I try to get to the track somewhere around 4:30."

There's no off-season in horse racing. "Vacation? There's no such thing in this

---

"Getting at it early is work ethic I learned on our Wisconsin farm..."

---

business. There's never a day when the horses don't need to be fed, cared for and closely observed."

So, 12 months a year, from California to Florida to his home track at Churchill Downs in Louisville, Wayne is one of the trainers who mounts a horse and rides onto the track early each morning to maintain his hands-on approach.

"After the workout, when the horse pulls up, I don't want an employee or exercise rider telling me that he went well," he explains. "I want to see how the horse is breathing, how tired he is, if he's rubber-legged. I want to be right there and see for myself.

"I demand a lot of myself and the others I work with. It's pretty intense, but it's allowed me to achieve some success. It's the work ethic I grew up with on a Wisconsin farm."

Students Be Aware

These days, "The Coach" finds himself competing against some of the very trainers he mentored. Many, such as 2010 Kentucky Derby winner Todd Pletcher, learned the tricks of the trade as one of his assistants. Wayne finds that highly satisfying.

"I'm sort of like the proud father," he chuckles. "I feel like Archie Manning with his sons Peyton and Eli. It's actually one of the things I'm most proud of—even more than winning a big race somewhere—to see these younger people succeed."

But if they do, Wayne isn't going to make it any easier for them. During his acceptance speech of yet another award recently, he finished his remarks with:

"When they start giving me awards, they're likely trying to get me to retire. Well, you young trainers better get up even earlier in the morning in the months ahead, because I'm coming after you just as hard as ever!"

Retirement simply isn't in his DNA. "Retire? Why would I do that?" he asks. "Why would I give up what I love to do?

"I told someone the other day I'll likely ride out there on my saddle horse one morning and just fall off, and that'll be fine. I don't have any intention of retiring in any way, shape or form. This is just what I do."

He's One Stern Taskmaster

A BARN FOREMAN of Lukas Racing recently offered this example of Wayne's management style.

"I noticed a protective bandage had slipped down a horse's leg and I was going to call a groom to fix it.

"Wayne said, 'No, don't touch it. Wait until 8 o'clock tonight when Jose's day is finished, he's had dinner and is watching TV in his room. Then go get him.

" 'That way he'll never leave the barn again with a bandage out of place. Better yet, if you wait 'til 9 o'clock when he's in bed, it will be even more effective.' "

Has a Softer Side as Well

TRAINER Dale Romans remembers seeing Lukas return to his barn after a race, not in a good mood after his favorite had just been beaten.

"But a few minutes later, I saw him standing out in the rain in a pricey Brioni suit, watching a young couple struggling to load an obstinate filly into their van.

"Wayne walked out there, adjusted the halter and shank, led the filly in three circles and it walked right into the van," recalls Romans. "He comes back in the barn and says, 'They were looking him in the eye. You can't do that!' "

He just may be Wisconsin's horse whisperer.

OPENING THE DOOR TO SPRING. Eagle Harbor in Ephraim is just one of many scenic sights in Door County. Ice cream at Wilson's (red-roofed building) has been a tradition since 1906. (Ken Dequaine photo)

A Dream That Became A Colorful Reality

Back in the 1930s, 200 men lived in tents and built a park enjoyed by thousands today.

NOW AND THEN. The Garden House, built in 1935-36 to resemble an early Wisconsin stone farmhouse, is still sturdy and in full use today.

CHARLES WHITNALL was a dreamer. As secretary of the Milwaukee County Park Commission in 1924, he dreamt of creating a place to serve as a retreat for city dwellers—where they could enjoy lakes, streams, trees, waterfalls, wildlife and flowers.

He didn't just dream, he acted on his vision. He pursued and succeeded in getting grants and help of the WPA (Work Projects Administration) and CCC (Civilian Conservation Corps). This yielded a crew of 200 muscular men—ages 18 to 25—from Milwaukee and Chicago.

Together they began the process of turning rolling farmland into a massive park, so large that even today an 18-hole golf course is tucked into a corner of it. The grounds encompass nearly 680 acres.

It was hard work for these men, who needed hand shovels, horses and strong backs to move boulders, walls and waterfalls. Together they created a series of parkways, buildings, rock formations, ponds and walking trails...they planted trees, shrubs, bushes and flowers...lots of flowers, which eventually included what is now one of the foremost rose gardens in the country.

Pay Was $30 a Month

The men lived in tents and ate in mess halls from July through December. They were then moved into barracks consisting of seven buildings. For all this, they were paid about $30 a month. Yet, with the shortage of jobs then, they were likely glad to find the work and surely must have been proud of the retreat-like site they were creating.

The result was Whitnall Park on the southwest corner of Milwaukee, a site so placid and peaceful it still lures thousands of visitors to the grounds, often many more than that each week during the summer when the vast rose garden is at its best.

Regular additions to the park have put it on the bucket list of gardeners throughout the country. In 1939, landscape artist Alfred Boerner created a 40-acre botanical garden. The site was later named Boerner Botanical Gardens in his honor, and in 1967 was selected to approve the All-America Selection flower trials. Today, the site is one of only 31 Trial Gardens throughout the U.S.

The Garden House, built by the WPA crew in 1935-36, is still sturdy and in use today. It features hand-hewn oak beams, a carved mantel and furnishings created by the artisans.

It has an oak parquet floor, and the

GARDEN GAZEBO was built by WPA carpenters using wood salvaged from farmhouses torn down during construction of Whitnall Park.

stone fireplace is made of native limestone cut from the quarry at Currie Park.

The current service yard and garage nearby was one of the original seven barracks that housed the workers.

Commemorated 75 Years

A lot happened last spring (2014) at the site, including the 30th anniversary of the "Friends of Boerner", a nonprofit organization that was created in 1984 to keep the community involved and this historic venue viable. All year-round, this support group is involved in community programming, fund-raising, student education and engaging community volunteers.

What's more, Whitnall Park commemorated the 75th anniversary of the efforts of a visionary who made his dream come true not only for himself, but also for thousands of garden enthusiasts who flock there for a "retreat" every year.

"CAMP WHITNALL". Third photo below shows barracks that housed 200 men in 1933-40. Top right shows beginning of now famous Rose Garden. Middle shows Peony Walk being built.

Merrimac Ferry— Older Than Wisconsin

This unique service has crossed the Wisconsin River for 168 years.

By Geoffrey Claridge
Sparta, Wisconsin

THE Merrimac Ferry provides such a novel experience that families headed north to the Dells are known to pull off I-90/94, head west to Lodi, then north to the ferry landing, where they're more than willing to wait.

Churning across the river is a unique delight for kids and parents. At the north end, they'll likely stop for a cone at the ice-cream stand, then head to the interstate.

Loss of an hour or more from their schedule? No problem.

It isn't just the ride they enjoy, it's the opportunity to connect with yesteryear. They know the ferry has been there "forever", but few are aware that the Merrimac Ferry is older than Wisconsin.

Merrimac's first settler, Chester "Matt" Mattson, obtained a territorial charter to provide ferry service across the Wisconsin River. It was 1844 and back then, river ferries were a Midwestern necessity.

Some 500 ferry charters were issued by legislatures during America's formative years. Matt and others hitched teams of horses to boats and pulled our nation in its never-ending need to get from here to there.

Throwback to Early Days

Today, modern highways and bridges have relegated the old river ferries to historical footnotes, except for the Merrimac. It's the last of its kind. The towlines still stretch across the Wisconsin River, and the direct descendant of Matt's ferry continues.

The Merrimac is the only free ferry service in Wisconsin. Since 1933, it has officially been part of State Highway 113 …make that, a *floating, moving* part of Highway 113. The ferry operates 24 hours a day from April through November, in all weather. The only thing that stops it is ice.

RIVER CROSSING. In the pilothouse, Martin Canales (right) captains the Merrimac Ferry. It takes only 7 minutes to cross the Wisconsin River on each trip—one that is repeated dozens of times a day during ferry season.

Photos: Michael Bie

The official name of the ferry is the "Colsac", an acronym of the two counties it connects: Columbia and Sauk.

In the pilothouse, some 30 feet above the river, Martin Canales mans the dual control panel—one for each direction. He throttles the boat into motion and sets the speed to cross the river. He slows at the approach, eases the boat into the landing, then lowers three ramps, one by one, to ensure an orderly exit by the vehicles. "Can't let them all off at once," he explains.

Martin returns a friendly wave to a traveler below. "We know a lot of people here," he says. "We recognize the regular drivers and wave to them every morning. In fact, when we see them coming from a distance, we wait."

The regulars even have their own signal—they flash their lights from the highway to indicate they'll be turning onto the approach, and the operators hold the ferry a minute or two to allow them to board.

The ferry can carry 15 cars or small trucks, plus as many excited kids as can line the railings.

It transports an average of more than 1,200 vehicles a day. The distance is a half mile across from Okee on the south bank to Merrimac on the north.

In a typical season of 8 to 9 months, the ferry will easily exceed 50,000 trips across the river, carrying more than 250,000 vehicles and passengers.

The ferry is faithfully operated by members of Columbia County's Highway Department. They're likely the only county highway employees in the nation charged with running a boat.

Highway on a Waterway

And the vessel they operate is in one of the most beautiful parts of Wisconsin. Travelers descend the bluffs on roads winding beneath canopies of trees, and cottages hug the shoreline among the evergreens.

Out on Highway 113, members of the Dandy Doers 4-H Club keep the road tidy. There are great places to eat in the area—supper clubs mark hamlets named Moon Valley, Harmony Grove and Pine Bluff.

Down on the river, eagles swoop above the water. If the timing is right, pelicans will be migrating through the valley.

The ferry's operator gazes out the pilothouse window at this scenery every day, and he never tires of it. Not even when he takes his turn running the late shift at 2 a.m. "Day or night," Martin says, "it's always so nice being down here on the river."

As he talks, headlights appear on the highway, then turn toward the landing. Martin throttles up the engine. As dependable as an old clock, the Merrimac Ferry is ready to make another of its crossings.

ALL EARS AND READY TO BOLT. Mike Crowley noticed movement in the tall grass near his Boulder Junction home, then this little guy popped his head up and played peekaboo.

Eileen Herrling

Joan M. Rood

SPLISH SPLASH. The joy of the spring season radiates from the face of Evie Williams, age 3, of Madison. Evie found this great mud puddle near the local zoo and thoroughly enjoyed it.

John Ford

WHERE'S THE ORANGE? On the bird, of course! This Baltimore oriole appeared near Greenwood, where the homeowner had not yet placed out any citrus in anticipation of its arrival. Orioles feed on fruits like berries, but also eat insects, particularly in spring.

REMEMBERING THOSE FALLEN. Lake View Cemetery in Oshkosh is dressed proudly for Memorial Day. Originally called "Decoration Day", Memorial Day was established as a national holiday by Congress in 1971, to be observed on the last Monday in May.

ROSE-BREASTED GROSBEAK is a member of the cardinal family that inhabits forests and forest edges. Wisconsin is at the core of its breeding range. This brilliant male was photographed not far from Greenwood.

RED FOX KITS start hunting with their parents when they're 3 months old. By 8 months, they are ready to strike out on their own. Wisconsin's red foxes are found across the state.

John Ford

Mark Wallner

Ken Dequaine

Lynn Stone

YELLOW LADY'S SLIPPERS bloom in the spring. Also known as "moccasin flower", these striking plants are common here and are one of the state's native orchids.

GREAT GRAZING. Apple blossoms frame these horses enjoying the warm sun and a grassy pasture near Valmy, in Door County.

Len Harris

TIGER HUNTER? Tainter Creek in Crawford County has been known to produce the rarest trout in the Midwest—the "Tiger trout", a hybrid of brook trout and brown trout named for its colors.

FIRST BLOSSOMS. The Vanguard variety of crocus says spring is here and brings delicate lavender color to the yard of Donna Krischan in Big Bend.

Donna Krischan

Lynn Stone

NESTING SEASON. A greater sandhill crane tends its nest in April, on a wetland edge in a pasture near Black Earth. The greater sandhill is the only subspecies of cranes that nests here.

Carol Toepke

RURAL HISTORY. The A.R. Potts Barn was built in 1902 near the village of Rural. The homestead was established in 1853. It's now the Crystal River Inn Bed & Breakfast, with gardens and restored prairie.

Mike Crowley

Jeff Halverson

AMBER HUES colored this sunny May morning in Janesville. Jeff Halverson of Oregon, Wis. says he spotted these backlit daffodils and just had to stop and take some photos.

THE EARLY BIRD. "I never feel that spring arrives in the Northwoods until I see my first robin, which is usually in early May here," writes Mike Crowley from Boulder Junction.

OurWisconsin

Zane Williams

MEMORIAL DAY HONORS. While driving through Fond du Lac on a pleasant spring day, Zane Williams of Madison spotted this flag proudly displayed on a porch. Zane stopped and spent a half hour taking pictures there.

Jeff Halverson

PEDALS, PLEASE! Vinny Halverson, age 2, is getting the hang of his hand-me-down tricycle on a sunny May day in Oregon, Wis. The trike is 40 years old and was once ridden by Vinny's mom, says his dad, Jeff.

BLOOMIN' BEAUTIES. Bird's-foot violets blossom in early spring at Kenosha's Chiwaukee Prairie. At 410 acres, this natural area is one of the largest prairie complexes in the state.

Brian Wolf

Carol Toepke

PELICANS IN SEARCH OF FISH. White pelicans were present in Wisconsin back in the 1700s and 1800s, but vanished. A resurgence in the 1990s happened on the Fox River from Lake Winnebago to Green Bay. These pelicans congregated in downtown Neenah.

113

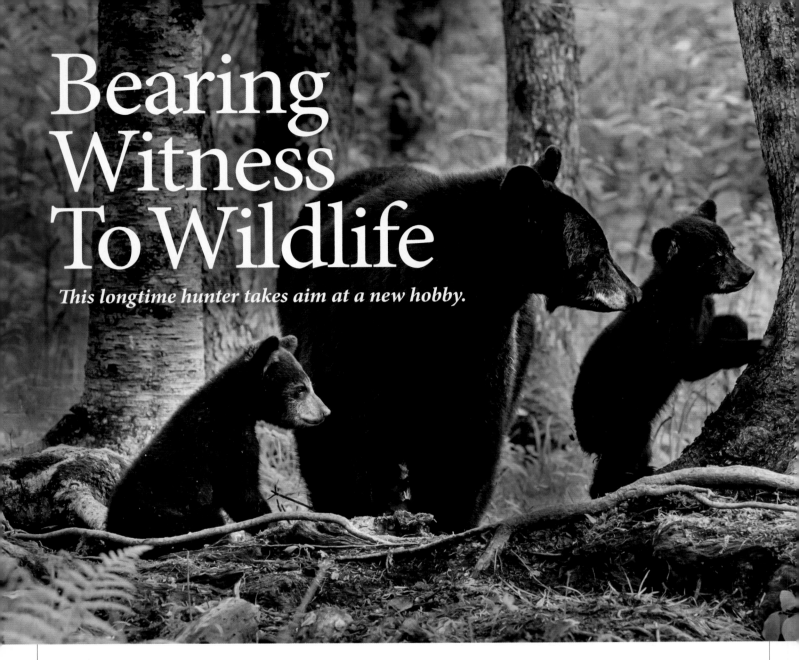

Bearing Witness To Wildlife

This longtime hunter takes aim at a new hobby.

By Nate Jackson
Pierce County Field Editor

SPRING of 2013 was highly unusual in northern Wisconsin, with deep snow lingering long into May.

Dave Shaffer of Washburn County well remembers that cold because it kindled a hot passion for a new hobby he loves: photographing black bears in Wisconsin.

"Yes, bears," he says. "I think they're a really neat animal…one that's often misunderstood."

When spring comes, bears emerge from their dens to find food, and that's generally in April. When a surprise late snowfall hit Washburn County last May, Dave encountered some bear tracks in the snow. He followed them and eventually caught up to a sow and her two cubs.

"The tracks led directly to a very cold mom with her scared and frigid cubs. I took a few photos but didn't spend much time there, so as not to put them under more stress.

"When the snow melted, I returned to that spot and found them again. As the weeks went by, I spent more time in this area waiting for photo opportunities."

Dave was raised as a hunter, and for years he successfully bagged game of all kinds with shotgun, rifle and bow. But that changed in 2012, when he began pursuing wild animals with his camera instead.

Same Skill, Different Goal

As a photographer, Dave was helped by all the skills he learned as an accomplished hunter: patience, awareness, observation, and the ability to remain quiet and still for hours at a stretch.

"This is way more challenging and rewarding," Dave says, pointing to the photos on his wall. "I now enjoy wildlife much more as an observer."

All Dave's photos of bears have been taken on public and private land near his home, most often at a distance of 10 to 50 yards. He uses a digital Nikon D-3S with a 200- to 400-millimeter lens.

"For every hundred photos I take, I hope to get one keeper," he says, noting that his best shots are taken on cloudy days because in bright sun, the black fur can give off a blue cast. He notes, "I love wet bears because it adds more detail to a photo."

Dave has learned it's virtually impossible to sneak up on a bear. They have one of the best senses of smell in any animal—experts contend it's *2,100 times*

BEARING UP under his tripod is photographer Dave Shaffer. Sow and cubs at left thrived in June, after he'd seen them during a cold May (cub at right). Top right: bear fur glistens after snow squall. Lower right is a young female.

better than humans. So his strategy is to allow the bears to get used to him being near. That can take 6 hours or more.

"It's also a matter of your energy," Dave explains. "There's no doubt they know I'm around, but I try not to put off a predator vibe. Instead, I remain as calm as possible, almost like I'm another bear."

Dave has found every bear he encounters has a unique personality. "They almost become predictable," he says. For instance, Dave noticed that one bear likes to walk on logs. "So I set out a log, and sure enough, he took a walk on it."

When asked the obvious question, about any concern he may have with bear attacks, Dave says, "I never get complacent; I always pay attention to my surroundings. Yes, they are wild animals and yes, things can go wrong. You need to be careful."

So when it's springtime in the Northwoods, you can bet Dave is out there pursuing his exciting hobby. It's clear his new focus—hunting with his lens—is far more enjoyable.

....

More of Dave Shaffer's photos are displayed at Naturally North in Spooner, Dancing Bird Art Studio in Cumberland and online at *bearwitnessimages.com.*

Vintage Views

Family-album photos offer a vivid look back at life in early-day Wisconsin.

THESE PICTURES from the past are shared to rekindle fond memories, as well as chronicle some of Wisconsin's distant history. There are many rich stories tucked away in family albums all across the state, and we print a few of them in each issue of *Our Wisconsin*.

So browse through your old albums and share cherished photos of family, friends or special events from the 1920s through the 1970s that help tell the story of Wisconsin's heritage.

Please include any information you have about the photo, such as the names of the people, the event pictured, location, year it was taken and anything else that explains why the picture is special to you.

To avoid loss or damage to your photo in the mail, we suggest having a high-resolution scan made of it before e-mailing it to: *editors@OurWisconsinMag.com*. Put "Vintage Views" in the subject line.

Or, make a copy of the photo and send to: "Vintage Views", *Our Wisconsin*, 399 S. Hwy. 51, Manitowish Waters WI 54545. Please include a self-addressed stamped envelope if you'd like the photo returned.

FAIR LADY WITH A FAIRLANE. Lynne McLernon from Lake Geneva was proud of her brand-new Ford Fairlane in 1955. Only 19 years old, she'd saved enough to order the car from a dealership...the first in her family to do so. When a friend saw the car, she remarked, "That's a honey!" So Lynne named her car "Honey Bear".

ORANGE-CRATE WAGON was shared by Tom Viney and Fran Swelle on a spring day in Green Bay in 1936. There was no room in the homemade wagon for Tom's older brother, Jack, who is standing.

FLOATING ALONG. A parade was held in Sheboygan on August 30, 1930 as part of a convention for the Wisconsin State Master Horseshoers and Blacksmiths Protective Association. Jerry Heisdorf of Elkhart Lake says his father was secretary-treasurer of the Modern Dairy Co-op, which was represented by this horse-drawn float shown on North 8th Street.

Shhh...the Morels Are Ready

Kary Nieuwenhuis/istockphoto.com

Mushroom hunters are secretive about their sites...take a walk with this reader to find some of your own.

By Rob Kruszynski
Green Bay, Wisconsin

SPRING BRINGS so much to us here in Wisconsin. Warm sunrises call our woodlands to life, with the return of greenery, the songbirds and the rich fragrance of good Mother Earth.

It's the time of year I treasure early morning hikes into my secret mushroom-hunting havens. Visiting them is like going to the "Church of the Forest"...it gives me quiet time to clear my mind.

Many people enjoy hunting for morels. The beauty of it is, morels are so distinctive, you don't need to be a mycologist to tell them apart from poisonous mushrooms. Morels grow in two varieties: black (dark) and blonde (like honey). They range in size from 1 inch to 10 inches in diameter.

There's a "false morel" that can be deadly, but it grows later in the year and looks deformed when compared with the typical morel.

The old-timers used to say the time to look for morels is when the oak leaves are the size of a squirrel's ear.

The best time to go is around Mother's Day, when temperatures are in the mid-50s to upper 60s, and when warm rains alternate with sunshine. The season is short—some years only 2 to 3 weeks, in other years as many as 6 weeks.

When I go (and I prefer to go it alone), I get up at sunrise and toss on a warm sweater, some old jeans and my trusty leather clodhoppers.

My list of gear is short: a pointed walking stick, a sharp pocketknife, a bottle of water. In a lightweight shoulder pack I carry a half dozen paper lunch bags and a few of the clear plastic containers used to hold supermarket strawberries. The air slots in these containers are useful because mushrooms must breathe. Avoid plastic bags.

I start looking in hardwood forests along sunny slopes with southern exposure. These slopes are best when damp from melted snow or rain. Another textbook site is around streams and wetlands where slippery elm trees grow.

It's also worth looking around orchards and in wet limestone areas. Door County is perfect for that.

When you walk into the woods approaching a suitable spot, *stop.*

This isn't a race, so pause for a moment. Then walk very slowly and examine the ground as if you're looking for some lost keys. Use your stick to carefully sweep branches and debris away. Remember...patience pays off.

Block Out a Pattern

One technique is to visually mark off a 10-foot by 10-foot block. Stand there and *slowly* look over each square foot in rows until you complete the block.

When you find your first mushroom, *don't move!*

Instead, squat down, take a few minutes to observe the area near that mushroom, then closely examine the entire block around it. Morels are like mice: when you see one, others are nearby. Locate as many as you can before you begin to gather them.

To harvest one, use your pocketknife to cut it off about a quarter inch above the ground. There may be a smaller one brewing from the same mass in the ground.

So watch where you step; you'd be surprised how many times one is right there.

Make mental note of where you were standing when you found the first one and return there once the block has been harvested. Now pivot around to examine the remaining 10-foot squares. Move along to the next worthy-looking area and repeat.

Once you've found your first morels and tasted them, you'll understand why they are an obsession. Served alongside pan-fried trout with bacon and a little pumpernickel bread...that, my friend, is lunch in the stratosphere. *Enjoy!*

A Simple Recipe for Morels

GENTLY BRUSH any dirt from the mushrooms. Lightly rinse in cool water. Use scissors to cut the mushrooms in half lengthwise. Rinse the hollow insides, then pat dry with paper towel.

In a well-seasoned cast-iron frying pan, melt a few teaspoons of butter (and a little garlic if you like). Do not burn the butter.

Add mushrooms, outsides facing up. Saute over medium-high heat for about a minute, until the butter melts into them.

Turn mushrooms and saute another minute or so, until they're slightly crisp. Finish with a pinch of salt (a coarse hickory-smoked sea salt works wonderfully).

Summer at Last...
So Much to See and Do

June...that's the month many of us have been waiting for. It's the true arrival of summer in Wisconsin, when we're eager to hop in the car to take in sites as well as sights.

Suddenly it's as though someone took crayons to our landscape—and it's all because June has finally arrived.

Wood violets (our state flower) are proudly spreading their hues on the hills...robins (state bird) are back in orange bunches...and our bright blue lakes (over *15,000* of them—far more than that state to the west) are beckoning us to get in them rather than just on them.

June warms our spirits and appeals to all the senses—there's an abundance of green fields, wildflowers and blue skies...shouts of children echoing across the lake...crickets calling in evening hours...and the unmatchable fresh fragrance after a mid-morning shower.

Hey, it's even barefoot time again! The garden's now in, the heirloom tomatoes are showing promise, and strawberries are ripe for the pickin'. Better hang the hammock, too, so when you're done with the gardening, you can do some deep thinking in the shade.

Baseball is back, too, for future pros such as that Little Leaguer at right. It's time, too, to paddle your own canoe, like one of those below.

For Wisconsinites, June's the time to whistle a happy tune.

Mike Crowley

"I'VE GOT IT, DAD." That's what Hunter Mieritz seems to be saying. Hunter's from Oulu, a town in Bayfield County so tiny it doesn't appear on most maps. But it obviously has a ball team...and a confident one at that.

Lindsay Hogfeldt

READY FOR SMOOTH CRUISING. Three canoes await the next group at a campsite along the beautiful Manitowish River north of Boulder Junction. That calm water is sure to be swirling soon! Rentals such as this are common in Wisconsin state parks, and we have 50 of those.

AT HEIGHT OF ITS GLORY. This 34- by 59-flag is proudly unfurled over the EAA AirVenture in Oshkosh by a member of the Liberty Parachute Team. (Rob Resnick photo)

PROUD PEDALER. Vinny Halverson is ready to ride in the parade at the town of Oregon's annual Summer Fest. His mom, Jenny, may have helped with the decoration job.

ANTLERS IN VELVET are seen in summer on Wisconsin whitetail bucks. Velvet is living tissue that supplies blood to antlers, allowing them to grow. In fall, when antlers are fully grown, they harden and the velvet falls off.

Jeff Halverson

Linda Freshwaters Arndt

Chris Schlosser

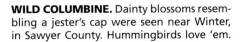

Linda Freshwaters Arndt

WILD COLUMBINE. Dainty blossoms resembling a jester's cap were seen near Winter, in Sawyer County. Hummingbirds love 'em.

LOST CREEK FALLS, near Cornucopia in Bayfield County, requires a hike to reach, but it's well worth the trip, says Chris Schlosser.

Carol Toepke

THE OLD BALL GAME was brand-new to Carol Toepke, who shot this photo on her first visit to Miller Park. "I love all of the colors, textures and patterns in this 'people-scape'," she says. Play ball!

MILKWEED FEEDER. A great spangled fritillary has lunch in a meadow. The striking butterfly is common in Wisconsin from June to September.

Linda Freshwaters Arndt

Linda Freshwaters Arndt

WHAT'S UP, PUP? Photogenic golden retriever paused for a moment in Birchwood. These little buddies are often full of energy, but like babies, they don't stay awake for very long.

Clint Farlinger

MAKING A SPLASH. These talented skiers are members of the Min-Aqua Bats water-ski club. They have entertained crowds of vacationers on Lake Minocqua for more than 60 years.

CANDY APPLE RED. This shiny 1950 F-1 Ford Pickup has been customized and is shown on display at the Cool City Classic Car Cruise and Show held each year in Two Rivers. Over 400 vintage car enthusiasts start at the UW-Manitowoc campus and drive the lakeshore to the "main drag" in Two Rivers for live music, food and fun. The 2014 event was the 14th annual.

Shana Shoblaska

Brian Wolf

PRIORITIES! Brian Wolf from Kenosha was loading the van to take the family to Miller Park when his grandson Isaac, age 1-1/2, heard the ice cream man approach. "He's quite a fan of the Brewers," Brian says, "but we did delay leaving until he'd finished his treat."

COLORFUL KAYAKS are part of the annual Park-to-Paddle event sponsored by the Fox Wisconsin Heritage Parkway. The "lock pack" at right happened in Menasha, as paddlers attempt to fill the lock with brilliant boats. The event happens in July. (Carol Toepke photo)

Eileen Herrling

FRIENDLY FOURSOME is playing Peninsula State Park Golf Course in Ephraim. Ralph Buesing, Bob Barlament, Gene Britton and Don Herrling enjoyed the scenic views during their round.

Rob Resnick

Jeff Halverson

A WIENER WHISTLE, PLEASE! The Oscar Mayer Wienermobile has been a crowd favorite since 1936. This model appeared at the Summer Fest celebration in Oregon, Wis.

LOOKS LIKE A BOBBER FROM HERE. Modern anglers may refer to these as "strike indicators", but Rob Resnick prefers the old-time term "bobber" and uses them to catch panfish.

Jeff Halverson

Jeff Halverson

GETTING HIS KICKS. Looks like the game's about to begin for this little soccer player, who competes in Oregon, in Dane County.

TASTES LIKE SUMMER. Picture-perfect ripe strawberries were handpicked at Wilfert Farms, founded back in 1877 near Two Rivers.

Shana Shoblaska

SUNRISE SWIM. A lone mallard has Lake Monona to himself on this serene summer morning. Jeff Halverson found some biting crappies that day on the Madison lake as well as the photo op.

Shana Shoblaska

NESTING OSPREYS use this platform near the East Twin River in east-central Wisconsin. This raptor was put on the endangered species list in 1972. It has since rebounded in numbers. Today, there are more than 500 breeding pairs in 49 of the state's counties.

ON THE FOLLOWING PAGES, Turtle Pond, in northern Vilas County, reflects tall evergreens and fair blue skies. (Mike Crowley photo)

125

Good Manners Are Par For Steve Stricker

The "pride of Wisconsin golfers" has never forgotten his Edgerton roots.

By Roy Reiman

THIS is a story about Steve Stricker the person, not Steve Stricker the putter.

Everyone who knows an eagle from a birdie is aware of his knack for reading greens and getting the ball in the hole when it counts...which is really important considering a 3-foot putt counts the same as a 300-yard drive.

Likewise, everyone associated with golf is aware Steve's the "Mr. Nice Guy" of the PGA Tour. Why, he even helped Tiger Woods with his putting prior to the tournament at Doral, then Tiger ended up beating Steve by two strokes. ...Or, make that two putts.

Some linksmen might have winced in retrospect. Not Steve. He said later he was glad to see his tips had worked for Tiger, and added, "All of us on the tour compete, but most of us are friends and don't mind helping each other now and then."

It's this kind of attitude and respect for others that has given him a revered reputation. Seldom do you hear broadcasters Nick Faldo or Jim Nance talk about Steve Stricker without adding something like, "He's one of the nicest guys on the PGA Tour."

To some degree, Steve owes it all to Edgerton. He formed his personality and his swing in that small town south of Madison, and in turn he's put that quiet burg on the national map.

Gladly Shared Memories

Most of the stories about his pro prowess have already been told. So, because Steve is "one of ours", this story's aimed at telling a bit of his roots and sharing a few personal happenings on his way to the pinnacle of pars.

We talked to a number of people, including his dad, Bob... Gene Haas, retired executive director of the WSGA (Wis. State Golf Assn.)...Gary D'Amato, golf editor of the *Milwaukee Journal Sentinel*...Dennis Tiziani, his coach (who's also his father-in-law)...plus club staffers at Cherokee Golf Club near Madison (where that now famous three-sided practice trailer is parked, the one Steve used to turn his game around by pounding out balls throughout the winter a few years ago).

And we got answers to non-golf questions like this: "How did Steve meet his wife, Nicki?"

Answer: He was walking with Coach Tiziani past the swimming pool at the course one day and said, "Wow! Who's the cute

---

"This 11-year-old kid kept dropping putts..."

---

new lifeguard?" And his coach said, "That's my daughter."

Amidst other memories shared, we learned Steve's good manners began at an early age.

"The first time I met him, I was running a junior tournament," recalls Gene Haas. "He was about 11 years old, just a skinny little guy, but very polite. He addressed me as 'Mr. Haas'.

"I was watching kids practicing on the putting green, and I noticed this one kid kept sinking putts. He stroked 10 to 15 balls from about 20 to 25 feet, and he dropped at least 75% of them.

"So I called Jack Reif over—he was the director of the Junior Program—and said, 'Watch that one young fellow putt.' It didn't

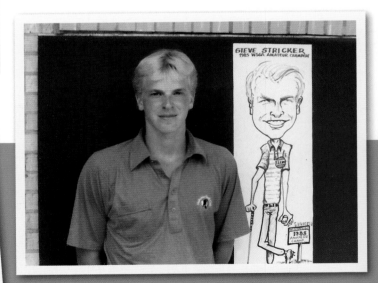

ALREADY A WINNER. This handsome young golfer was walking off with trophies at an early age. Here Steve is shown after winning the State Amateur Championship in 1986. The caricatures were drawn by Gene Haas, a longtime Wisconsin golf administrator and fine golfer as well.

take long before Jack was just standing there shaking his head, too; the boy just kept dropping 'em.

"Another time, I was helping with a junior tournament at Rivermoor in Waterford. Late in the day, some of the players were still on the course, so to fill time for the early finishers, we decided to hold a driving contest. So this same kid comes up and asks, 'Mr. Haas, can I get in that driving contest?'

"I checked his name tag and said, 'You sure can, Steve.'

"And then he asked, 'Do I have to hit it from the same tee as those big guys?'

"The tournament was for boys up to 18, and there's quite a difference in size between 11 and 18. But I said, 'I'm afraid you do. It's the same tee for all.'

"Well, my assistant, Paul Becker, stationed himself exactly 200 yards down range to mark the balls—we didn't have laser beams for measuring in those days. Each player got to hit three balls. And when this little Stricker kid hit his first drive, it rolled right past Paul's left foot, at 201 yards.

"He hits the second ball, and it rolls past Paul's right foot about a yard farther. And when he hit the third, it went between Paul's legs and stopped at 210 yards!

"He didn't win the longest drive, but we were amazed at his accuracy even then.

"A few years ago, I was talking to Steve—this was when he was having problems with his driver—and I mentioned how I remembered those three drives when he was just 11 years old. He laughed and said, 'I wish I was that accurate now!' "

Caught Nicki's Eye as Well

When I related the story about Steve noticing the cute lifeguard at the pool, Gene said, "Well, actually that went both ways. Steve caddied for Mario Tiziani, Dennis' son, who was a really good golfer, too.

"Steve was a good-looking young guy, and Mario's sister, Nicki, obviously noticed. And I soon noticed she started hanging around more when Steve was caddying!"

Steve and his older brother, Scott, got started in golf at an early age partly due to convenience. The Towne Country Club

State's Top Golfing Couple?

STEVE'S WIFE, Nicki, is a great golfer in her own right. She played on the women's team for 4 years at the University of Wisconsin, and in 1992 she recorded a round of 70.

That was the lowest score ever recorded by a woman golfer in the Big Ten. And that record still stands today.

She's since won the Madison City Women's Tournament several times, with Steve as her caddie.

When asked whether Nicki gives any advice or suggestions to Steve these days when she sometimes caddies for him on tour, her father said, "I think she's mostly a stabilizing source for him. She knows the right things to say and when.

"But mostly she remembers the code of every caddie: 'Put up, keep up, shut up.' "

was within easy walking distance from their Edgerton home. So they headed there with their dad—an avid golfer—on weekends and after work during the week.

And work they did. Their dad was an electrician, so they pulled wire and handled whatever tasks needed. During his high school years, Steve worked at the local lumberyard, then caddied on weekends to earn college funds.

His athletic abilities weren't limited to golf. He excelled in tennis and basketball, too, while playing for Edgerton teams.

But golf soon became his passion, and it resulted in a

TALENTED TEEN. Steve may wince a bit when he sees we used this photo, but this was "the look" when he won the 1985 State Junior Championship at Bull's Eye Country Club in Wisconsin Rapids.

THE "COMEBACK TRAILER". Steve is shown here working on bunker shots from the three-sided practice trailer he uses during winter and early spring. After slipping a bit in the PGA ranks a few years ago, he worked particularly hard on his driver, hitting hundreds of balls onto a snow-covered range the following winter.

from the University of Illinois. Many people aren't aware that Steve was named to the All-American college golf team three times. When Gary D'Amato noticed those three trophies while visiting the Stricker home, Steve typically made light of it in sort of an "Oh, that" fashion.

That kind of modesty and good manners have continued to be part of his makeup. When Gary was writing a book about

"Now, how many other professionals would do that?"

putting, he called Steve to see if he'd be willing to help with a photo session. After a quick okay, Gary agreed to meet Steve at Cherokee Country Club.

"It was a cold day in March," Gary recalls, "and Steve showed up in deer hunting clothes. I asked him if he wouldn't mind changing to golf clothes; he said sure and changed in the clubhouse.

"We started shooting the pictures, and because it was important to show the position of the hands and arms, I asked if he'd take off his long-sleeved jacket. No problem.

"Now, it's only 35 degrees, and the photographer is staging picture after picture, and I can see Steve is getting redder and redder. I asked if he'd like to stop and warm up, and he said, 'No, let's just get this finished,' and we were out there for another half hour or so.

"When we finally wrapped up the photos, he said, 'C'mon inside, I'll buy you guys lunch.' Here we'd taken up well over an hour of his time, he's out there posing in freezing temperatures and he buys us lunch! Now, how many other professional athletes would do that?"

Gary shared another example of Steve's regular-guy attitude. "He's had problems with his neck, and I mentioned to him that I have the same problem; in fact it's the very same vertebra as his.

"I didn't see him for 3 months after that, until I was covering the John Deere Classic. Steve spotted me across the room and the

EARLY SPRING TUNEUP. The specially made practice trailer Steve uses is located at Cherokee Country Club near Madison. It has accommodations for various types of shots, including sand play. It's used by Wisconsin PGA players Jerry Kelly and Andy North, and some local club members as well.

first thing he says is, 'Hey, Gary, how's your neck?'

"I was amazed that he remembered and cared enough to ask about it. That's just the kind of person he is."

Fortunately, now that Steve has slowed down a bit (he says he's in "semi-retirement"), he's extending some of this same care to his own family. Recently he didn't return home from a tournament until 2 a.m., but he still got up to take his two daughters (Bobbi, 14, and Isabella,"Izzy", 7) to school.

"I'm now doing a lot of things around home with the family," he said recently. "I go to the grocery store with Nicki, we go to basketball games together, the regular stuff.

"I think this lighter schedule is helping my demeanor on the golf course as well. I told Nicki if I can just make enough money to cover our yearly expenses as a family, I'm fine with that. I'd rather spend more time at home."

"Home" is still Edgerton, with easy access to hunting and fishing (he's even adept at landing muskies—he caught several measuring over 50 inches last fall, and daughter Bobbi landed a 47-incher). And when the weather turns bad, he can still work on his game in that three-sided trailer at Cherokee Country Club.

None of the "Mr. Nice Guy" image surprises his father-in-law, Dennis, who has known and coached Steve since he was a teenager: "He treats the guy working in Aisle 4 at Home Depot the same as he treats the big executives on tour. It's just the way he is."

That positive image is good for the state of Wisconsin. It reflects the kind of people who live here.

We're all fortunate to have Steve as an ambassador...a guy who's as much about politeness and appropriateness as he is about putting.

He's One Up on Tony

GOLF isn't Steve's only game. He's apparently still good at shooting buckets as well.

According to his father-in-law, "Steve's the only guy I know who ever beat Tony Bennett in a game of H-O-R-S-E." And that was just a couple of years ago.

Wisconsin sports fans know Tony is the son of former UW basketball coach Dick Bennett. While at UWGB, Tony was a shooting guard and still ranks first in NCAA Division 1 for 3-point shooting accuracy—49%!

Tony later played in the NBA with the Charlotte Hornets and is now a successful head coach at the University of Virginia.

But he's one down in H-O-R-S-E with Steve Stricker.

RED SKY AT NIGHT...anglers' delight. These fishermen enjoy a peaceful close to a spectacular day on Lake Winnebago, the state's largest lake. (Aaron Jors photo)

SHORE IS BEAUTIFUL! Where is everybody? Not even the water is moving in the harbor at Sister Bay on a picture-perfect summer day. (Ken Dequaine photo)

Who Knew Wisconsin's a
HORSESHOES HOTBED?

There are pits aplenty across the state...and tournaments with a lot at stake.

By Jim Haupt, Milwaukee, Wisconsin

CLANK! Everyone's heard that distinctive sound when a flying horseshoe meets a metal stake. And then comes the joyful shout: *"Ringer!"*

Casual players have fun with this game in backyards and parks all over Wisconsin. But what most people don't know is this state is a hotbed for horseshoes as an organized sport—and it has been this way for nearly a century.

In the 1920s, men played games alongside the smithy's shop. As these games became popular, neighborhood clubs formed. Pitchers would build a set of courts, then get together one evening per week to play.

In Milwaukee, they formed the Sycamore Club, The Auer Avenue Club and the Washington Park Club. Horseshoes flourished in this city, where it took but a streetcar ride to get to the game. The downtown Milwaukee Athletic Club, catering to the more affluent, had courts on the roof.

Often thought to be a game straight off the farm, horseshoes fast became a metropolitan man's sport in Wisconsin. The National Horseshoe Pitchers Association was organized in 1919 in Florida.

Crowds Paid to Watch

Across the Midwest, expert pitchers barnstormed the countryside to play before paying crowds. The sport was new to many, and they yearned to be part of it.

In 1923, the Wisconsin State Fair in West Allis saw an opportunity, installed courts and offered space to hold a state tournament. The 1948 World Horseshoe Tournament was conducted on these courts.

Most state champions of the period hailed from Milwaukee and Waukesha. State Fair Park was the site of the state tournament for 42 years.

Out in the smaller communities of rural Wisconsin, the game flourished as well and continues to be popular today.

The Fox River Valley community of Combined Locks was first to hold the state tournament outside State Fair Park. Jerry Kamps, a tavern keeper in "the locks", expanded his facility to conduct the tournament. You might call it an early sports bar. Today, Kamps Kovered Kourts has eight courts under one roof.

Biggest in Beloit

There are many active and welcoming clubs in the state, and the largest of them is in Beloit, with a tournament schedule that rivals all others combined.

The Beloit Horseshoe Club built 13 courts outdoors, then added an indoor horseshoe house of six courts plus a club room. Offering 17 tournaments, five outdoors and 12 indoors, the Beloit Club creates the most horseshoe action in the state. It's a destination of choice for most Wisconsin pitchers throughout the year and also attracts a good number from Illinois.

Horseshoe pitchers are a friendly bunch, willing to help and encourage all comers at any skill level. As you'll see from the list below, there's a club not far from you. Leagues are a good starting point, ongoing May through September in all locations.

Give it a try and make someone happy …and don't be surprised if that someone turns out to be you yelling, *"Ringer!"*

Horseshoe Pitcher's Paradise

HERE are places where you can give organized horseshoes a try:

Arkdale: The Adams County Horseshoe Club has (arguably) the best sand in the state and hosts tournaments in July and August. Sand pitchers, put Arkdale on your list.

Centuria: It's a small town, but big on horseshoes. The annual Wet 'n' Wild Tournament held the first weekend in September attracts many good pitchers from nearby Minneapolis.

Deansville: A great place to play when the snow flies. The Deansville Horseshoe Barn,

IF THE SHOES FIT... These do fit the fancy of avid horseshoe pitchers who travel to all corners of Wisconsin to compete in every season. It's not just a game for summer picnics anymore!

not far from Sun Prairie, has four indoor clay courts in a modern metal building.

Eagle River: The Headwaters Horseshoe Club, which plays on four nice sand courts at the Vilas County Fairgrounds, hosts a tournament in May. If you also like fishing, May is a perfect time to visit!

Eau Claire: The club here meticulously cares for 18 outdoor courts in Carson Park. Eau Claire held the state horseshoe tournament on nine occasions over the past 48 years and has twice hosted the world tournament.

Fond du Lac: The oldest continuously operating horseshoe club in the state, it has an extensive court layout on the fairgrounds where the state tournament has been held several times.

Green Bay: Visit their tournament in August at The Watering Hole sports bar. Indoor and outdoor courts at this facility keep the play happening in every season.

Germantown: The Goldendale Club, in operation since 1972, has six courts in a nice setting. Enjoy some good league play here at the Lone Star Tavern. The club holds one annual tournament.

La Crosse: The pitching here is unique, done on sand called slate. It resembles material on a baseball infield. Head to La Crosse and give it try!

Marengo: Located 13 miles south of Ashland, in a lovely region of the state, they hold a tournament in early September as part of the Ashland County Fair.

Marshfield: The 13-court layout here has hosted a state tournament. Their annual tournament happens each June around Father's Day.

Mosinee: The Little Bull Falls Horseshoe Club plays two tournaments on newer courts outdoors, and indoors at a hockey facility.

Muskego: The Moose Lodge has plenty of sand courts. Many champions have pitched in their annual tournament on Father's Day or thereabouts.

Platteville: The play happens here in Legion Park on clay imported from Dubuque, Iowa. They have many courts and have hosted several state tournaments, most recently in 2009.

All are cordially invited to participate in these clubs and events. For information, contact the Wisconsin Horseshoe Pitchers Association, *whpa.tripod.com* or 414/964-2735.

Quips From Wisconsin Kids

istockphoto.com

KIDS from Wisconsin are the same as all others—they say the darnedest things! In each issue of Our Wisconsin magazine, we feature a few sent in by readers. Here are some samples:

WHEN our son Dean was small, my husband attended a postgraduate session at UW-Madison. He left the house on Sunday nights and returned on Fridays.

Every Sunday little Dean would cry. *"Why?"* he'd sob, "why do you have to go to college?"

"I go to college to learn and get smart," my husband would answer. "You want Daddy to be smart, don't you?"

The teary-eyed 4-year-old looked up and said, "No, I don't want you to be smart. I want you to be just the way you are." —*Janet Werry, Muskego*

WE WERE traveling from our home in Port Washington to visit some relatives near Eau Claire. We mentioned to our granddaughter Cindy, 4, that we were going through Wisconsin Rapids.

After driving through the river communities, we rolled back into the country. Soon Cindy began to cry. "But I didn't see any!" she bawled.

When we asked what she hadn't seen, she sobbed, "Wisconsin rabbits!" —*June Wulff, Franklinton, North Carolina*

WHEN our daughter got married, the photographer came to our house before the church ceremony. He posed her in our yard, standing near a tree.

I learned later that during the photo session, our neighbor happened to drive by. She told us her 4-year-old granddaughter took in the scene and said, "Grandma, look, that lady is marrying a tree!" —*Mae Dricken, West Bend*

MY NIECE Carol was 3 and had been dropped off to spend the day with my mother.

For an afternoon snack, Mom gave Carol a bunch of green grapes. When she finished eating them, Carol said, "Here, Grandma...you can take the antlers." —*Marjorie Bengston, Madison*

WHEN my granddaughter Breanna was in grade school, she took golf lessons. One morning she worked her way through the course, and sometime near noon she landed a ball in a sand trap.

After several swings, her coach asked, "Do you have a sand wedge?"

"No," she replied, "but I am hungry." —*Sue Schmitt, Green Bay*

GRANDDAUGHTER Abbie, age 4, was enjoying an ice cream treat with us. Her mother cautioned her not to eat it too quickly, "or you will get a 'brain freeze'."

Abbie decided to share her ice cream with Grandpa, and each time she spooned it to me, she asked, "Do you have a brain freeze?"

"No, not yet," I kept saying.

After her third or fourth attempt, she finally said, "Grandpa, I don't think you have a brain." —*Gary Wodack, Sturgeon Bay*

GNARLED SENTINEL. This twisted juniper tree stands watch from an overlook of the Wisconsin River Valley near Lodi. (Zane Williams photo)

Typewriter Inventor Held Keys to the Future

To this day, the 1868 keyboard remains an integral part of personal computers, tablets and smart phones used worldwide.

By Mark Michaelson
La Crosse, Wisconsin

EVEN IF he hadn't come to be known as the "Father of the Typewriter", Christopher Latham Sholes would have a prominent place in Wisconsin history. A printer by trade, Sholes came to this territory in 1837, when much of it was still a howling wilderness.

Milwaukee

He'd come from Pennsylvania at age 18 to help two older brothers publish a Green Bay newspaper. After a later stint at a Madison newspaper, Sholes moved to the Kenosha area and became owner and publisher of his own journal—*The Southport Telegraph*—at age 21.

It was a wild and woolly time on the frontier. In 1842, Sholes witnessed a heated argument between two members of the territorial government in the council chambers over who would be appointed sheriff of Grant County. That debate ended when one member shot the other dead.

In the 1850s, Sholes moved to Milwaukee to work on Republican newspapers. He visited Wisconsin troops during the Civil War, reporting back to Governor Edward Salomon.

Despite interests in politics and journalism, Sholes' true love was tinkering with things to make them work better.

Wisconsin Historical Society

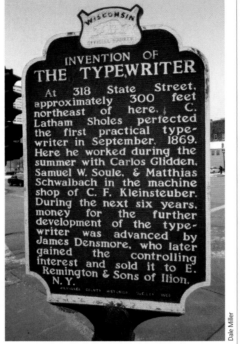
Dale Miller

COMMEMORATIVE PLAQUE at corner of 4th and State Streets in Milwaukee marks location of the building where Christopher Sholes (below left) perfected his invention.

As one writer put it, "With his tall, emaciated figure, his flowing white hair and beard, his whimsical ways and dreamy look, he fitted perfectly the popular conception of an inventive genius."

Addressed a Problem

Tired of writing subscribers' names and addresses on the margins of newspapers, Sholes created a device that stamped that information automatically. He spent much of his time at C.J. Kleinsteuber's machine shop at 4th and State Streets in Milwaukee, a sort of mecca for amateur inventors. It was there Sholes began work on a typing machine, inspired to do so by an article in *Scientific American* about a machine invented by an Alabama man.

That prototype, made of wood, was described as "a cross between a kitchen table and a small piano". Instead of levers for the keys, it used wires, but the basic premise—keys made of single letters that struck a sheet of paper in front of an inked ribbon—was present from the beginning.

The keyboard evolved many times before it became the familiar "QWERTY" keyboard of today. Almost all early keyboards had the keys in alphabetical order, but such machines jammed too often. The solution, he found, was to separate frequently used keys; this reduced the stuck keys problem. That's likely the reason he settled on the QWERTY configuration.

Tried Out by Twain

Sholes and his chief financial backer, James Densmore, formed a company to market the machine, but it took years for the world to realize its worth. Ironically, Sholes himself never thought the machine would amount to more than a curiosity. That sentiment was shared by Mark Twain, who, after purchasing one, called it "a curiosity-breeding little joker".

Sholes would eventually sell his interest in the company for roughly $25,000. Meanwhile, Densmore eventually made a fortune after selling the machine to the E. Remington & Sons Company—the same company that made firearms.

Still, the typewriter didn't take off as a tool until after 1888, when a Michigan law clerk named Frank E. McGurrin won a typing contest with an invention of his own—a touch-typing technique. Before then, only the two-finger "hunt-and-peck" style had been used.

Others claimed to have invented the typewriter, since machines to put words on paper had been built as early as the 1700s. But Sholes is credited as the device's father because his machine was the first one durable enough and efficient enough to be mass-produced.

Although Sholes died in Milwaukee in 1890, his typewriter enjoyed more than a century of popularity before being replaced by the word processor.

Meanwhile, that QWERTY keyboard created in a Milwaukee machine shop lives on in modern computers, tablets and smart phones—a durable testament to the genius of a Wisconsin tinkerer.

Mike Roemer   Carol Toepke

"SHAKE THE LAKE" is hydroplane racing at its best, with boats making tight quarter-mile laps. Event took place on Millers Bay, on Lake Winnebago, in Oshkosh.

THOSE LAZY DAYS OF SUMMER surely suit this group of happy teenagers. What's not to like about summer in Wisconsin?

GOOD MORNING...SAFE PASSAGE. Sunrise warms the Pierhead Lighthouse at the Sturgeon Bay Ship Canal. Built in 1881, this light guides ships traversing the canal between Lake Michigan and Green Bay. (Mike Roemer photo)

A Few Fluttering Facts About

Butterflies

You touch its wings, it can't fly? Wrong. There's more to learn about these flittering eye-catchers, and how to lure their beauty to your backyard.

Laurie Painter

MANY NATURE LOVERS look at butterflies as virtual "flying flowers" that bring dancing colors and interest to their flower gardens.

Susan Borkin looks at them much differently. She not only appreciates their beauty, she *understands* them.

She knows what colors do and don't attract them...what they like to eat and how they do it (basically through a "straw")... that Wisconsin is home to over 100 species of butterflies...and a whole lot more.

No wonder. Susan is curator of the Puelicher Butterfly Wing at the Milwaukee Public Museum. She gives visitors a whole new appreciation of these lovable insects—yes, they are insects.

To begin, here are some "hits and myths" about these winging wonders:

✿ *If you touch a butterfly's wings, it will no longer be able to fly.* Your mom was wrong; that's a myth. It can still fly, but touching should be discouraged, because that removes scales from the wings.

These scales not only give the butterfly its unique color pattern, but for some species it helps to camouflage itself. Without it, it can no longer blend in with plants and hide from predators.

So, touching a butterfly's wings is not a death sentence, but it can affect its ability to fly as effectively, as well as display appropriate patterns to a potential mate.

✿ *Butterflies are attracted to the color red.* Nope, not true, either. So if you're planting red flowers to attract them, it won't hurt, but it likely won't help. There are other properties to flowers that catch their attention; the color red just isn't one of them. That isn't to say they aren't attracted to any colors, because butterflies are thought to have the widest visual color

range of any living species. But it varies somewhat by species. Butterflies are attracted to the colors of their mates, and to define them they use color patterns not visible to the human eye.

✿ *When butterflies flit around you or light on you, they're being friendly. Bzzzz!* Wrong again. In some cases, these "flying flowers" are very territorial. So when one lands on your head or shoulder, you may think, *Ah, what a special moment!* When, in fact, the butterfly would actually prefer you leave its territory.

✿ *Butterflies actually have two pairs of wings.* Even if it was your mother-in-law who told you this, she was right. Unlike

---

"Landing on your head doesn't really mean it likes you..."

---

the transparent wings of dragonflies and bees, butterfly wings feature a variety of colors and patterns. These colors are created by thousands of tiny, overlapping scales, much like the scales on a fish.

✿ *Some butterflies appear to have four legs.* Actually they have six. Only four are fully developed and used for perching and walking. Don't ask your mom why. Even Susan doesn't know.

✿ *The mouth of a butterfly is basically an advanced straw.* True. It consists of two separate tubes that are interlocked like the teeth of a zipper to form a feeding apparatus. Hmmm...baby butterflies must need to learn to drink from a straw quickly.

✿ *Butterflies have a pair of straight, clubbed antenna, while moths have a*

feathery antenna without "clubs". True again. Amazingly, the moths' antenna is so receptive that male moths can detect chemical signals from females several miles away! Bet your mom didn't know that. ...But then this piece is about butterflies.

How to Beckon These Beauties

We asked Susan for advice on how to attract more of these eye-catchers to your backyard, and also asked for suggestions from Nathan Brockman, one of the top butterfly curators in the Midwest. Here's what we learned:

✿ Butterflies prefer sunny rather than shady locations, especially those protected from the wind.

✿ They're attracted to plants that supply ample nectar. Here are some of their favorites: black-eyed Susan, coneflower, hyssop, lantana, milkweed, salvia, verbena and zinnia.

✿ Use a diversity of plants that flower all season, and include plants of different sizes. Plants with narrow stems and large flowers for a "wide landing pad" are beneficial.

✿ They prefer a lawn that isn't mowed too closely. Some species feed on grasses or weedier plants as larvae.

✿ Reduce pesticide usage if possible.

✿ A good water source is an attraction.

✿ If you have a fruit tree, leave some of the rotting fruit on the ground for butterflies to feed on.

Finally, here's a fun fact Nathan shared: Butterflies use a feeding strategy called "trap lining", which means they visit the same plants each day in the same particular order. So, if time allows, you might see if your flittering friends follow that pattern.

Good luck in luring more of these beauties to your backyard!

SUMMER SOLITUDE. Kayaker is enjoying the view of the stunning red sandstone of Devils Island. It's part of the Apostle Islands National Lakeshore on Lake Superior. (Aaron Peterson photo)

THE DELLS OF EAU CLAIRE. "This park is one of our favorite places to explore," says Carol Toepke. "But don't be fooled by the name, because it's in Aniwa, near Wausau! The waterfall is a product of the Eau Claire River and is pretty any time of year. The rocky gorge provides a series of miniature eddies formed by the swirling water." (Carol Toepke photo)

Wisconsin...There Are So Many Sites to Be Seen

"SIGHTSEEING" is popular in the Badger State. Little wonder, with so much beauty that's there for the lookin'...from Prescott to Sturgeon Bay, from Beloit to Presque Isle and all in between.

Sightseeing even qualifies as a "class" for school groups, such as this one shown above on a field trip enjoying an overlook of the Mississippi River.

They're likely counting the cars of that train chugging over the bridge...while their teachers are pointing out the time and effort it took to build tracks across that large body of water.

And maybe they're telling these youngsters that these wooded areas look much the same as when French explorer Jean Nicolet landed in Green Bay in 1634.

Judging by the colors and foliage, it's likely this field trip was taken in June, the month many residents have been waiting

for. It's the true arrival of summer in Wisconsin, when we're eager to load the kids in the car to take in sites as well as sights.

Let Your Fingers Take the Tour. If you're planning a trip across the state in the months ahead, you might want to go back over the preceding pages.

Some of the state's top photographers captured all those colorful images, and they share scenes you'd likely never find on your own. They've traveled to all corners of Wisconsin to help you "visit" a lot of neat places and neat people.

So you can use their pictures and details as a guide to find sun-splashed country backroads...the top of bluffs and mini mountains...and hidden lakes deep into northern woods. In many ways, this book is a "Wisconsin Almanac".

Does a Gift Come to Mind? We spent weeks selecting only the best photos

and articles from the first 2 years of *Our Wisconsin* magazine, and added a bunch of entirely "new" material as well.

We hope you enjoyed our selections, and that you might share your copy of this book with your family and friends.

Better yet, we hope you'll consider ordering a gift copy for a family member or friend, for a birthday, anniversary or just a "Thinking of you...thought you'd love this" gift.

And if you haven't already subscribed to *Our Wisconsin*, we hope you'll consider that as well, so we can "come to visit you" every month through its bimonthly issues. You can do so either by phone or e-mail —see details on page 5.

With that, thank you for spending time with us via these 148 pages, so that together we can celebrate this spectacular state we so proudly call...*Our Wisconsin*.